memoir and poetry to create something that feels raw and unfiltered."   —Shannon Carlin, *BUST*

"[A] poetically punk debut memoir about ancestry, loss, colonialism, rebuilding, power, hope and healing."
                                    —Karla J. Strand, *Ms.*

"[LaPointe] offers up an unblinking reckoning with personal traumas amplified by the collective historical traumas of colonialism and genocide that continue to haunt native peoples. *Red Paint* is an intersectional autobiography of lineage, resilience, and, above all, the ability to heal."
                                    —*Shelf Unbound*

"[A] cutting, artful thrashing of settler colonialism and a sensitive exploration of ways of healing and forging space for community and connection through storytelling . . . LaPointe's intimate prose is introspective, raging and funny . . . [She] explores her experiences and familial legacies in a wash of rage, beauty, love and reclamation of strength via storytelling."   —*Shelf Awareness* (starred review)

"Although the author does not shy away from heartache and sorrow, readers are welcomed on what is ultimately a healing journey that will stick in their memories. An engaging, poetic, educative examination of the search for home and personal and cultural identity."
                                    —*Kirkus Reviews* (starred review)

"*Red Paint* is an ode to healing and to healers, told by someone who intimately knows both. Steeped in punk music and poetry, it is an ode to Indigenous inheritance and to the work and wisdom necessary to recover from the legacies of trauma. It is the truest kind of love story: one in which every lover is a MacGuffin, propelling its narrator toward the person who matters most—herself."

—Melissa Febos, author of *Girlhood*

"*Red Paint* is a miraculous book. Sasha LaPointe walks us through the sites of her evisceration while rebuilding a home within her body using sturdy materials: rose quartz, cedar bark, red clay, and the words of her ancestors. With each potent sentence, she shows us what access to power looks like. She shows us how to become whole."

—Elissa Washuta, author of *White Magic*

"As luminous as the morning sun over the fir forests, *Red Paint* is a story of where strength takes us. Sasha taqʷšəblu LaPointe goes looking to the past to help heal from terrible traumas, finding inspiration in her ancestors, the Salish people. This is a book destined to be a classic. Read it."

—Rene Denfeld, bestselling author of *The Child Finder*

"*Red Paint* offers a poetic narrative of trauma and healing through ancestral rites and punk rock, both of which prove to be potent medicine during LaPointe's excavation of family legacy and matrilineal power."

—Catherine Hollis, *BookPage*

"[A] stirring debut . . . LaPointe writes in lucid vignettes that alternate between past and present as she reflects on her ancestors, Salish medicine workers who 'faced violence, disease, and genocide' . . . LaPointe's fresh and urgent perspective on Indigenous culture is enthralling."

—*Publishers Weekly*

THUNDER
SONG

Also by Sasha taqʷšəblu LaPointe

*Red Paint: The Ancestral Autobiography
of a Coast Salish Punk*

Rose Quartz: Poems

THUNDER SONG

Essays

Sasha taqʷšəblu LaPointe

COUNTERPOINT
BERKELEY, CALIFORNIA

Thunder Song

First Counterpoint edition: 2024

Library of Congress Cataloging-in-Publication Data
Names: LaPointe, Sasha taqʷšeblu, author.
Title: Thunder song : essays / Sasha taqwšeblu LaPointe.
Description: First Counterpoint edition | Berkeley : Counterpoint, 2024.
Identifiers: LCCN 2023041698 | ISBN 9781640096356 (hardcover) | ISBN 9781640096509 (ebook)
Subjects: LCSH: Coast Salish Indians—Ethnic identity. | LCGFT: Essays.
Classification: LCC PS3612.A64394 T49 2024 | DDC 814/.6—dc23/eng/20231010
LC record available at https://lccn.loc.gov/2023041698

Jacket design by Nicole Caputo
Jacket illustration © Maynard Johnny
Book design by Laura Berry

COUNTERPOINT
2560 Ninth Street, Suite 318
Berkeley, CA 94710
www.counterpointpress.com

Printed in the United States of America

1 3 5 7 9 10 8 6 4 2

Vi taqʷšəblu Hilbert believed in the healing power of music. She believed in our ancestors' Coast Salish spirit songs. My great grandmother wanted to share that medicine with the world, in the hopes it might teach us something. She wanted us to be better. She passed that hope down to me.

This book is for her, and for anyone who is ready to listen.

The essays in this collection were written with care and respect. Not all the stories or experiences that appear within this book are solely mine to tell, but they are told through my own lens and experience of them. Some names have been changed or intentionally left out to protect families and their privacy. Any events and experiences shared are done so with care and compassion, with the hope they might reach readers who can relate, and readers who can learn something from these stories.

Contents

※

THUNDER
SONG

Siʔaɫ: Orations: 1

I n 2001 my great-grandmother set out to commission the writing of a symphony. She was persistent, determined each time she called the Seattle Symphony offices only to be told there was absolutely no way her request would even be considered. *We have stacks of proposals that sit taller than the desk*, they told her every time before saying goodbye and hanging up on her. Each time, she called back a week later and asked how it (her symphony) was coming along. My eighty-three-year-old great-grandmother would not take no for an answer. She believed in the healing power of music, of song. She believed it needed to happen and to happen immediately. She didn't give up. When the Seattle Symphony could no longer resist the charm and determination of our great-grandmother, they told her yes. They had to. So Grandma began work on what would become *The Healing Heart of the First People of This Land*, a work to be performed in four parts by an orchestra at Benaroya Hall. She gave the composer two cassette tapes to listen to, one of which held Chief Seattle's spirit song.

I remember feeling validated when she made the announcement to the family. Music had always been important to me. When I was just a kid, I'd hover over a boom box in our trailer's small bathroom. I'd hit record on the cassette deck. Stop, rewind, play, stop, then record again. I was making mixtapes. I was daydreaming, lost in a city miles away from the woods I felt buried in. I fell in love with bands, with haunting melodies and the howl and gravel of a stranger's voice. I wanted to be part of it, this wave of music in the nineties that crashed into the Pacific Northwest like a tsunami. But I was a kid. I was on a reservation. What did I know of the world, of music, of anger?

Years after the trailer, that bathroom, and those mixtapes, I stood in front of a bronze figure, lamplit in the streetlights of Belltown. I had just come from a punk show, from a loud and rowdy venue deep in the city. The kind of place that the child me out on the reservation had only ever dreamed of. After the show my friends and I sat at the 5 Point Cafe eating French fries, and I, feeling restless, wandered outside to pace, to watch my breath fog patterns against the dark. I noticed the statue instantly and crossed the street. I studied the curve of his rib cage, the length of his metal arm outstretched, hanging just above my head. Looking at his face, etched in copper lines, eyes frozen staring ahead, I couldn't help but recall those stolen moments in the bathroom, those mixtapes, how I longed to be here in his namesake city. As I looked up at his bronze likeness against the night sky already scarred with starlight, I remembered my great-grandmother's words. How she believed our Coast Salish songs and stories could heal something. I read the carved placard below: CHIEF SEATTLE. FIRM FRIEND OF THE WHITES.

I closed my eyes and heard her voice as she told us, "It's pronounced siʔax̌', not Seattle. Not Sealth.

"Siʔax̌'."

Thunder Song

I n 2006, I watched my great-grandmother address a sold-out crowd at Seattle's Benaroya Hall. She climbed the wooden steps of the stage, her small frame draped in her wool shawl, and I watched as her father's painted drum was handed to a percussionist in the orchestra. My great-grandmother, my namesake, turned and addressed the audience. She spoke about the first people of this land. She talked about a need for healing. "People," she said, her heart breaking for a wounded world, "have lost their way." Her father's drum sounded. The first powerful beat reverberated like thunder.

Fourteen years later, my mom sits at her desk, a mosaic of script pages laid out around her. She's studying the opening scenes, the interviews, and the movements of the music. She's finalizing what will become the documentary of my great-grandmother's symphony. She looks up from her tiles and tells me, "This must happen now. People need to hear this music again." The footage for the documentary has sat unused, dormant for all these years. Until now.

That spring, at the height of the COVID-19 pandemic, police officers murdered George Floyd in the streets of Minneapolis. Protests erupted around the country, and cop cars burned in the streets of Seattle.

My great-grandmother was eighty-three years old when she commissioned *The Healing Heart of the First People of This Land*. She had been troubled by the world. Back then, in 2001, the news was all about George W. Bush's war on terror. She saw beyond the fear. She saw a country divided, the wars across the ocean and the violent injustices in her own streets. She saw that the people had lost their way. She believed so deeply in our people's stories, the teachings inherent in them. She knew that no one would listen to an old Indian woman, that she would have to reach them another way. Somehow, she arrived at what she called highbrow music: symphonies. This came as a shock to us. My great-grandmother hadn't grown up with this kind of stuff. She loved square dancing and Elvis. But she believed this was the way, that if all people could experience our beliefs through song, the music could heal the wound. She needed something that everyone could hear. She called a famous composer. "I need you to write a symphony," she demanded, "and to perform it at Benaroya Hall."

The composer turned her down.

But weeks after the call, he couldn't get this eighty-three-year-old Indian woman's voice out of his head. He called her back and together they collaborated on a symphony, the first to be based on Coast Salish spirit songs with lyrics in Lushootseed, the traditional language.

In our longhouse ceremonies, songs hold a spiritual power. There are certain songs for prayer, for healing. My great-grandmother had a cassette tape with recordings of two spirit songs: one belonged to a beloved cousin, and the other was Chief Seattle's thunder spirit song. She entrusted the tape to the composer with instructions to listen to but not share them. She wanted the songs to guide him as he wrote the symphony. She hoped that the healing power of these spirit songs would take shape in the symphony and that when people heard it, they might be touched by that power. She was hoping for medicine, for a world that could change.

On a hot summer day in 2020 I stood thronged in protest, in collective grief and anger. We yelled, we chanted, we demanded justice. I raised my cardboard sign that read in bold letters INDIGENOUS SOLIDARITY WITH BLACK LIVES MATTER. But it didn't feel like enough, would never feel like enough.

Weeks went by. Weeks of flash-bangs and tear gas. Weeks of protesters being arrested and assaulted, until finally the people took over the precinct. With the police gone, the organizers secured six Seattle city blocks, declaring it the Capitol Hill Autonomous

Zone. There were medical tents and tables of free books on political education. People brought crates of food to share, while others held demonstrations. My partner and I walked the streets of a free Seattle, watching films being projected onto buildings, seeing murals painted over boarded-up windows. There were large plastic bottles of hand sanitizer duct-taped to telephone poles.

It seemed as though the people had created a utopia. Until it didn't. We turned a corner to find the park in the center of the autonomous zone in full-blown festival mode. Kids in droves wielded glow sticks. It looked like Coachella. It looked like Burning Man. People were drunk, waving selfie sticks instead of placards, wearing angel wings and carrying Hula-Hoops. *Is this what change looked like?*

But in the middle of the intersection, we found a gathering of Coast Salish people. I watched as men laid out large cedar boughs in a circle. Then women entered carrying burning bundles. The cedar smoke wafted over the crowd, the tents, the abandoned precinct. They were sharing their medicine.

When the first speaker approached, he asked that any and all Coast Salish and indigenous people come forward to the edge of the circle. He asked that the white people step back for us. I looked at my partner, who looked at me, then gently let go of my hand. A young woman stepped away from her girlfriend and together we both stepped forward, away from our white partners.

"Before we begin here today," the man with the mic yelled, "I want to honor our elder Vi taqʷšəblu Hilbert. It's important we remember her, here on her land, for the work she did for the Coast Salish people." The man spoke in Lushootseed and in English. He introduced a group of Coast Salish singers. They made a half-moon around the burning cedar and hit their drums hard. I closed my eyes and saw my great-grandmother as she stood on stage at Benaroya Hall fourteen years earlier. I saw the painted drum, heard its heartbeat as it boomed like thunder, as it called out for change. I hadn't heard my great-grandmother's name, her Skagit name, the name we shared, spoken in a very long time.

The symphony had been her last project; she passed away before the documentary could be made. But right up until the end she went to gatherings, to speaking events, events like this. I had seen her small and frail but still so powerful when she spoke. I thought of her here today in this crowd and shuddered at the imagined worry. Even amid the threat of this pandemic, she would have been here. I let the drums wash over me as I cried, transporting me to the smoke-filled longhouse, my great-grandmother's hand on my shoulder as we listened.

—

Throughout this pandemic I return to the books my great-grandmother made, the ones that house our language and our stories. Some days I spend crying, curled in the crook of my partner's lap as the cats and dog wander the house, charged with an animal anxiety. Some days I make salmon and black coffee, simply to fill the house with the familiar aroma of my great-grandmother's kitchen. All these white women on Pinterest are baking loaves of sourdough, and I am trying to time travel.

We climb out onto the roof of my house and watch the sky change. The world has stopped, but it feels even more frozen on the reservation. I have good days and bad days. We make a game out of our once-a-month grocery shopping. We call it the Hunger Games. We call it the Soft Apocalypse as we wait in line outside the Trader Joe's, masks on and six feet apart from everyone but each other. We dress up at night, light all the candles in the house, eat the fanciest meal we can muster, and drink wine like expats in Paris.

We spend the summer locked inside, only able to be outdoors for fifteen minutes at a time. Beyond that it's too dangerous, as the smoke from the wildfires ignites my asthma. I boil pots of cedar and rosemary to help me breathe. And still people are dying in record numbers. We are losing our elders and I try to find my breath. I look for a mountain I can no longer see, its peak enveloped in smoke. A thick blanket of haze conceals the islands I know are out there dotting the waters beyond the shore.

On election night my partner and I sit barefoot on the floor, nervously checking our phones. We scroll. We put them down, then anxiously pick them up again. We do this until I can't take it anymore. "How is this even an option?" I hold up my screen showing the very close count. I am afraid as a Coast Salish woman, a female-bodied person, a queer person. I am afraid for the people still being murdered by police, for the elders still threatened by the pandemic. I am afraid for how many times I might have to endure another aggression from a person who refuses to wear a mask but still clings to their MAGA hat like it was a prayer. Would I feel safe again? Would the world feel safe again? My partner picks up his guitar and strums the opening chords of one of my favorite Ramones songs. I join in off-key and giggling. By the time we reach the chorus we are hysterical, barely able to get the lines out. We make it through the song only to roar with laughter and begin again. There is a power in the repetition. We let the song transport us.

In her own home on election night, my mom is not scrolling the news. She is pressing play, pause, and rewind, busy transcribing interviews, busy sorting through the raw footage of that day at Benaroya Hall. Again and again, her grandmother illuminates the screen, paused in smile, in speech. Occasionally the music floats through, the symphony inspired by a Coast Salish spirit song. In the interviews my great-grandmother talks about her anxiety for the world, her rising concern, but there is something confident in her smile, some glimmer of hope when she speaks about the power of song.

"People have lost their way," she says. "They need to be reminded to take care of one another."

There is a belief in my Coast Salish culture that songs have the power to heal, that they can be medicine. My great-grandmother wanted to share that knowledge, she wanted to remind people to have compassion, she wanted to change things. I don't know anything about symphonies or orchestras. I don't know any spirit songs. But as we sing out loud until two in the morning on election night, we are no longer checking our phones. We are not thinking about the president or the pandemic. We are laughing, lost in the music, lost in trying to get it right, lost in a brief moment of hope. We are singing, we are dancing.

We are trying to heal.

Si?aƛ': Orations: 2

***There was a time when our people
covered the land as the waves of a
wind-ruffled sea cover its shell-paved
floor.****

They say Chief Seattle was a protector, that he
shielded his people from the threat of attacks
from neighboring tribes. He led with wisdom.
He led peacefully, strategically. He had a voice that
carried, that boomed like thunder. According to his-
torians, he spoke before the governor at a gathering
in 1854 to address the surrender and sale of Native
land to white settlers. There's some controversy over
the written record of Chief Seattle's famed speech.
There are different versions. The most well-known
comes from Henry Smith, a young white doctor
who was present at the gathering and transcribed
the speech from Lushootseed to English. His tran-
scription showed up in print thirty years after the
Duwamish chief delivered it.

I find it difficult to trust a text that has been transcribed and rewritten in the colonizer's language.
But when I read it over, what I find isn't surrender

but courage. It isn't rage but grief, or love, or both. I think Chief Seattle saw something the others didn't. The shrinking of his lands, his people. I try to imagine what it must have felt like to see that in real time, to watch your loved ones, the people charged to your care, become ghosts.

—

Once, when I was a teenager, my father and I were talking about *America's Next Top Model*. There were agents scouting a nearby mall for possible contestants. A friend of mine was standing in line, awaiting her chance to be discovered. *It's so gross*, I exclaimed, *so horribly toxic, reinforcing harmful beauty standards. Sexist. Misogynist. Wrong.* My father and I had seen the same article, something praising the show for its inclusion of black, Asian, and Pacific Islander models, of *nonwhite* models. *Still*, I argued, *it's bullshit. It is*, my father interrupted me. *There are no Native Americans on Next Top Model*, he said, and in one sentence erased everything I had previously been angry about. Just moments before, I had been angry about the male gaze, about objectification. I stood silent, jaw agape as he continued, *They don't think to include us because they don't remember us. They don't even know we exist.* I had never even considered this. It was 2003.

—

The most Indians I've ever seen in one place were the homeless ones begging for change in Pioneer Square. That's their village now. A white man said this to me casually at a bar in South Seattle. He didn't know, because I didn't tell him: he was in the presence of an Indian. To him, my light complexion made me safe, unassuming. He continued as I turned my back to him, gripped the cold metal tap and poured his beer. *I won't give them any money. They're just gonna spend it on booze.* And I had to bite my lip so hard it felt like it might bleed. And I turned to him, and said nothing, set his pint down, charged him for two instead of one, because he wouldn't notice, because I needed the money.

Chief Seattle's bronze statue is 1.8 miles from Pioneer Square.

Tulips

*Few pioneers in the history of our country ever at-
tempted to build homes in a more uninviting region.
The people of the older settlements of the sound
thought it absurd to try to claim such a* **desolate
tide-swept waste.** *At high tide, the Indians
paddled their canoes wherever they wished over
what are now the finest farms in Washington.*
— The Pioneering of the Skagit

*Tulips weren't introduced to the United States un-
til the mid-19th century and not to Washington
State until the tail end of the 1800s, thanks to a
man named George Gibbs. Gibbs, a settler from
England, made his way to the States at the age
of 17 and settled in the Puget Sound on Orcas Island. He originally intended to grow apples and
hazelnuts, which he did in 1883* **on 121 acres
of land that he leased for some $10 a
year.** — A Brief History of the
Skagit Valley Tulip Festival

wrote a new song. Kari's text lit up my screen, followed by the bell chiming as the audio file came
in. *Do you have lyrics?*

Not yet, I responded, *but I know it's called Tulips.* The word had been caught on a loop in my head. I couldn't get the vision of petals and colors out of my mind. I didn't know how or what I wanted to say about the flowers, just that I couldn't stop thinking about them. I put my earbuds in and listened to the song on repeat as I hiked down into Swan Creek. I listened again and again until words eventually floated up.

Violet, yellow, red, cover tidelands.

In the summer of 2011, I went with my mother to the Swinomish Canoe Journey celebration and grand opening of the tribe's Swadabs waterfront park. The site is located in the ancestral village of Txiwuc. I had just come home for summer vacation after my first year away at college in New Mexico. I was homesick. When she invited me, I hesitated. Returning to Swinomish was complicated for me. But I wanted to walk along the water, to spend time with my mother, and to see the paddlers. The day was hot and bright. We greeted relatives and walked the newly manicured trails in the park. I could see the field across the street, could hear the songs as they rose up. Beyond the field stood the longhouse, and behind it the tall trees of my childhood home. The mood was light and celebratory. People smiled and talked excitedly to one another. We came to three pavilions in the center of the trail, the park's main attraction. They were designed to look like our traditional cedar woven hats and I stood in awe of their beauty. It was a moment of pride.

All the years I spent growing up here, it always struck me as sad to imagine the white town of La Conner, just across the Swinomish channel in all its picturesque, postcard perfection, looking over at our reservation roads. La Conner was a town made up of art galleries and ice-cream shops, antique stores, and waterfront restaurants that boasted the world's best fish-and-chips. I knew the view from the fanciest fine dining restaurant on Main Street. I had sat there before, at the big picture window that looked out across the water and right onto the reservation. I remember seeing the old fishing boats and fireworks stands put away for the season. I remember wondering if the diners gave us a second thought as they enjoyed their seafood and prime rib, or did the view annoy them? The way poverty can muddle an ideal vision of Pacific Northwest beauty. Perhaps once it was shame that curled its way through my body when confronting the view of my childhood home, but as I grew older it shape-shifted into questions, then eventually into anger.

But as I stood before the three pavilions along the water, I smiled at their splendor. I hoped that the tourists could see us gathered on the beach, proud and celebratory. Inside the large cedar woven hats were three panels, murals painted by my artist aunt.

They were stunning. In vibrant shades of dark green and deep blue, my aunt depicted the land as it was before white settlement. As I studied the waterways and the people in canoes, the camps along the beach, it occurred to me I had never even considered what the land might have been before. The place between the waterfront village I grew up in and the town of Mount Vernon had always been what I knew of it, farmhouses and fields, cow manure and miles of cultivated crops. When I stared at the painting the farm flats disappeared, replaced by rich marshes and tideflats. Waterways and reeds made up the land. Looking at my aunt's painting, the only flowers I could find were the occasional wild blossoms on a berry bush or native plant. I had never imagined a time when the valley wasn't marked by its famous flower. That day I saw the world through my aunt's eyes, through our ancestors' eyes. Tulips have haunted me ever since.

The first memory I have of being really late to something was on account of tulip traffic. We were on McLean Road, between La Conner and Mount Vernon. I was nine and in the back seat with my siblings as my parents fought the traffic to get us somewhere important, a wedding maybe, some event where punctuality was crucial. To get from our home on the Swinomish reservation to the town of Mount Vernon, the drive takes twenty minutes. To get there you have to traverse the farm flats of Skagit Valley and cross the river. On a good day you can do the drive in eighteen minutes. This day it took my family an hour and a half, maybe longer. All I really remember was the anxiety in the car; the frustration was palpable. I can still hear the long sighs of my parents, powerless in the gridlock. Through the density of tour buses and crowds of visitors all clamoring to see the famous Skagit Valley Tulip Festival, I could see an ocean of color. Every field was a sea of bright pink, fuchsia, violet, or red. It didn't look real.

That same year I remember getting in trouble so bad it sent my dad into a rage, shouting and throwing every piece of furniture around the small bedroom my sister and I shared in our single-wide trailer. He screamed and wrecked the room. He slammed the door, leaving me in the aftermath to clean it up and to think about what I had done. But at nine years old I couldn't really understand what had broken inside my dad. It was a rage too big for a kid to grasp. I was in the third grade and a girl from our class invited me to come over and play at her house after school. My sister and I were the same age, and together we walked down our gravel driveway and a quarter of a mile through the woods on Indian Road to meet my new friend. Hannah's family was white, possibly the only white family living on Indian Road, and they didn't live in a trailer like we did. Their house was huge and made of wood. They had a large yard with bright green grass and flower boxes. It looked out of place. When we arrived, Hannah came out to greet us with a somber look. She explained she had only asked permission to have one friend over, and I shamefully sent my sister walking the quarter of a mile back home alone. I don't remember what Hannah and I did that afternoon or how we spent the time. We didn't stay friends. But when I arrived home my parents were furious.

At first, I thought it was because I had made my sister walk alone. But as my dad shouted and tore the room apart, I listened to his words. As my T-shirts and toys rained down in a violent storm, I learned it was because my sister is darker skinned than me. It was because I am a light-skinned Coast Salish girl. I'm half-Indian and therefore have the privilege of passing in white spaces. In racist spaces. My dad cursed and yelled. The family had let me stay on account of my complexion and sent my sister home because she was Indian in an obvious kind of way. *White people will treat you differently than your sister*, he said to me, *because you look more like them*.

The memory of Hannah's mother, her silhouette in the window as my sister and I approached their home on Indian Road, stayed with me. Then Hannah telling us only I could come inside, and me telling my sister I'd meet her back at the trailer, stayed with me. The way their house looked in comparison to our own stayed with me. The way it didn't fit or belong. If

I close my eyes and think long enough, I swear I can remember tulips in their planter boxes, bright red and purple against the dark trees. I remember something wedging itself between my sister and me, and it cracked something in me. As a kid I wasn't even sure how to ask for forgiveness for something like that, for not knowing the ways white people would see us as different. I worried my sister might never see me as a sister again, until—after the incident and because I was grounded on Christmas—my sister snuck out into the woods and dragged back the biggest branch of a fir tree she could carry and pulled it in through our bedroom window. She stole ornaments off the tree in the living room and brought Christmas right to me. We never spoke about Hannah or that walk back on Indian Road.

The water that cuts through the valley separating Swinomish from La Conner is narrow enough to see across. These two communities are in close proximity but worlds apart. It's living on the edge of a knife, it's a pot almost always but never quite bubbling over. The high school we all got funneled into was in La Conner proper. There was no tribal school on the reservation. I can still see the painted mural as you drive in from La Conner Whitney Road: La Conner Braves. This was the team.

After the incident on Indian Road, I became aware of all the ways this moment occurred again and again in the split community we shared: An afternoon hitchhiking at fourteen, when the driver eyed me, then instructed my brown friend to *get in the back*. My light-skin privilege afforded me the front seat, where for the eighteen-minute drive into town I was rigid with worry. Or the days spent walking through the gated community on the reservation, a place named Shelter Bay, where white people leased land from the tribe, where the fancy houses dotted the tree line along the beach, where eventually my parents were able to move us to, and the ancient white security guard would nod as I passed by, shaved head, blue lipstick, backpack full of illegal substances, then like clockwork would stop my younger brothers, just a few yards behind me. *Where you boys going today?* He did this each day, like the answer would change. I learned to preemptively shout *391 Queets Place. They're with me.* Every time. My brothers, like my sister, have different mothers from me. They are darker than me. Never mind that we are family, that we all live in the same household, are all tribally enrolled; never mind that my brothers had backpacks full of classwork and skate videos and things far more wholesome than I did. Never mind that I was a card-carrying Indian and way more of a delinquent than my brothers would ever be. The security guard felt safer letting me through the gate because I looked more like him.

It is hard for me to wrap my brain around the idea that white people fear the first people, the original stewards of the land they now occupy. It's hard to understand where this hatred comes from. I think of children who have done something bad, broken or taken something that doesn't belong to them. More often than showing remorse or feeling apologetic, the misbehaving child simply leans into their tantrum. It's difficult for me to process the anger I feel when white people, friends, forget to or, worse yet, refuse to clock me as Native. It's backhanded racism that feels like an erasure. A friend once told me at a party that she had a really bad day. She got off her shift at a bar and as she walked the dark streets of downtown a man had harassed her. *Ugh*, she rolled her eyes and shook her blond hair dramatically. *You know how it is, all those drunk Indians down there, it was awful.* My *friend*, who knew me, who knew I was Native, still seemed shocked by my angry, defensive reaction. I raised my voice and puffed out my chest, afraid for a moment of my own rage, of the fact that I might fight her right there in the kitchen. *You know that I am Native*, I challenged. But she just smiled apologetically and, like it was nothing, like it was no big deal, responded easily, *Yeah, of course I know you're Native, but you're not like that.* There was an emphasis on *that*. And I had to excuse myself from the kitchen, from the party, because I was exactly *that*. In that moment I was a drunk and angry Native. I was all of the things she was afraid of. To her I just didn't look the part.

In movies I've seen a recurring narrative, a formulaic plot rooted in the simple idea that new people come in and change some beloved space. Whether it's a precious record store going corporate or an old farmhouse getting a hideously modern makeover, the villain, the new guy, comes firing in hot with big plans to change things, to erase what's been and create something new. We see this again and again. It's crazy to me that white people devour this tired narrative in their movies but refuse to see it in the reality of their settler status. The settler's residency on our land comes from a generational violence that is passed down through ancestry. And as if this were not crime enough, what angers me is the denial of that history and its replacement with entitlement.

To be entitled you must first feel worthy. There must be a sense of pride. I think back shamefully to my days at the La Conner elementary and middle schools. First there was Hannah, who asked me to dismiss my sister and ushered me into the reality of racism, which led me to question everything. Then there were other friends and crushes. There were the white lies to my white classmates—*I live over there*, I'd say and point in some ambiguous direction. I lied about living on the reservation. I took my charade so far at age twelve that I even had a white skateboarder, a tourist on vacation with his family, walk me to the gate of someone else's house. A stranger's house. I recall the gate and the painted mailbox, the hanging flowers that curled their vining tendrils around our first and only kiss. I was so ashamed of the place I lived, where the streets were littered with trash and abandoned vehicles. I was ashamed of my home, of my *Indianness*. When I learned that white people would treat me differently on account of my light-skinned Nativeness, I unknowingly learned to slip in and out of their projection like into and out of an ill-fitting costume. Every time I did this—lied about where I was from or didn't let a friend walk me all the way home—I was participating in their erasure of what was here before. I changed the landscape of my own identity the same way settlers changed the land they took from us.

The settlement of Skagit Valley dates back to the mid-1800s. Fur trade routes brought an influx of people to the San Juan Islands and eventually to the mainland. One of the first claims would become March's Point. This was Swinomish territory, and the land was bought for sixty dollars and a gold watch and given to a white man. The first homesteaders found the environment disagreeable. Salt marshes and tideflats made the land difficult to settle. But when they discovered they could dike, then drain, their watery claims and transform the tidelands into fertile fields for farming, more and more settlers arrived. Once they knew they could reach beyond the hills and prairies, that their reach could extend into the tidelands, the early settlers opened a world of rich possibilities. In diking the waterways, they created the most fertile farmlands in the Washington Territory. They cultivated hops and barley. They logged the mountains that surrounded the valley, and industry boomed across my ancestors' homeland, leaving it forever changed.

In my aunt's paintings the land is mostly water. There are no dikes and farmhouses, no stretching fields of crops. But there is an abundance. My ancestors maneuvered the waterways in canoes, they made camps along the beaches. They gathered shellfish and harvested berries and fished salmon from the river. They understood something about the land; rather than needing to carve it into something else they learned to move with the supply of resources. When I think of what the settlers had to do in order to make this their home, I think of it as cheating. They took something beautiful and wild and broke it, like taming a wild animal.

Over a hundred years after the white settlement of Skagit Valley, the first Tulip Festival was held here. An English settler, George Gibbs, had discovered that the flower bulbs did exceptionally well in the newly diked rich soil. Ninety years after Gibbs's discovery, the first Tulip Festival was held in 1984. Eight years after that inaugural festival I sat in traffic on an old farm road as my parents tried to find an alternate route, some way around the masses of tourists who stood between a Native family and their destination.

My family learned to adapt to the festival every
year. Each spring we knew for one week in April not
to make plans that involved driving to Mount Vernon. We learned to cushion appointment times and
to plan accordingly. A twenty-minute drive became
two hours. Mostly we stayed home, we stayed at
Swinomish, until the hordes of tourists emptied out
of the valley and gave us back the land.

Growing up against the backdrop of a colonial
celebration isn't easy. You learn to move through a
landscape of erasure without ever even realizing it.
Sure, we hated the tulips as teenagers but for different
reasons, reasons that barely skimmed the surface of
the wound. My friends and I worked service industry
jobs, and the festival brought wave after wave of tour
buses to our small town. The street fair was three
days of pure hell and it happened right out front of
the Skagit Valley Food Co-op, where I worked. It was
an endless barrage of serving coffee and giving out
directions, of people shouting and fighting to get their
orders. Outside was a nightmare of funnel cakes and
screaming children and white people wearing tulip
shirts and fawning over local crafts. After our shifts
we'd climb out onto the fire escape and smoke cigarettes as the moon rose over the empty waterfront.
The streets below were finally quiet and deserted, all
but paper cups and littered trash rustling along the
pavement. My friends would groan and crack open
a bottle of dark ale, complaining about the day, the

tourists, how we'd have to do it all again tomorrow. I'd look out over the water, toward the reservation, not realizing in that moment how invisible I felt, some lonely erasure moving through my body. I wouldn't speak it aloud, but some part of me always remembered my dad's voice, his rage as he said the words. *They will treat you differently because you look more like them.* People throughout my life, my white friends, strangers, see what they want to see when they look at me. I have been asked *What are you?* and told *I always thought you were part Mexican.* And *You don't look white, but I wouldn't have assumed you're an Indian. You look part Asian. I thought you were part Korean. Really, Native American? But how much? What percentage?* When non-Native people have made Indian jokes in front of me, they laugh like it's nothing, because shouldn't it be? Because they feel safe enough to make these jokes in my presence. Because they see what they want to see, and what they see erases me. It erases history.

Coming back to Skagit Valley as an adult I know now that the anger and frustration was never about the traffic jams or the crowds. It was not the hand-crafted folk art and the watercolors of brightly colored tulips. I see the rows and rows of flowers spanning the valley in a rainbow of color. That valley was once our ancestors' tidelands, their waterways, their place of harvesting and abundance. The tulips happen every year, a petal-made flag of settler colonial triumph, a reminder that we have lost something.

Tourists wait for unimaginable lengths of time just to step out into this vastness of color. They pay a fee in order to snap one photo and caption it *It looks like a dream*. Last spring my friend and I waited until nightfall to drive out to the tulips. We broke into the flower fields when no one else was there. It didn't look like a dream but a gravesite. Or a monument. Something was once here. And now it's gone. The white people who settled this valley broke it and bent it to their will. They transformed flooded tidelands and marked the valley in flowers, in something they wanted to see. What was once, according to the settlers, a desolate, tide-swept waste is now an ocean of flowers, soft and pretty in the moonlight. These flowers are safer than salt water and rocks, and narrow channels and reeds, and fishing or drowning, flooding, freezing, starving, dying, disappearing. The flowers bury all the things my ancestors understood about surviving here. When I look at their petals, I think of how far they are from their native fields, but here they are nonetheless, thriving. I think of Hannah's house on Indian Road, the small channel that separates the reservation from the town. I think of the fear and the frustration and the hatred between white people and Indian bodies. It is easier to look at this valley blanketed in cultivated color than to consider that once it was wild. That what is here is here because it erased something. Like my Coast Salish face, it's easier, because of my mixed ancestry. *They will treat you differently because you look more like them.* Because my tidelands have already become tulips to them.

I haven't been back to the tulip fields and will likely never go again. But this summer I hiked on the Kukutali Preserve at Swinomish. A friend, who is also a relative, had moved back. *The land was calling,* she told me, a smile big on her face as she looked out toward the salt water and the islands floating on the horizon, dense with tall cedar trees. We climbed the trail through the wooded hills, then down to the beach. As we walked my relative asked me, *Do you ever feel at home when you walk out here on the land, along the water? Like how our ancestors must have felt.* When we reached the water the shells that made up the beach crunched and cracked beneath our boots. The waves lapped lightly at the shore and I took a deep breath, gratitude swelling up like the tide in me. The Kukutali Preserve is protected by law now. This place in the Swinomish territory can never be bought or sold or owned. My relative's words resonated with something inside me, something that bloomed in the emptiness that was once there, the parts of me that ever wished to deny this land and this water. I'm thankful for her. Thankful she's back on her ancestral lands, happy, thriving, making music and singing, telling her story.

At my home in Tacoma last spring, I walked out onto my porch in the morning with my coffee.

I laughed when I saw them there: Over two dozen tulips had sprouted in my garden. Violet and red, yellow and orange. I hadn't planted them and wondered which roommate had, or perhaps they had always been there; like Gibbs's bulbs, they had multiplied and sprung back with a vengeance. I laughed so hard I almost spit out my coffee. I made a deal with the tulips, offered them a treaty. They could stay here in my garden. They could be reservation tulips. And I picked all of them over the weeks and made bouquets for my friends. It was an opportunity.

This summer I sang "Tulips" for the first time. In the garage, Kari and I tore through the song again and again in order to get it right. The first time I tried to yell into the mic I was flooded with emotion. Kari's guitar was loud enough and she didn't see as I turned to face the wall behind me, crying hard and heavy as I screamed into the mic. And it wasn't grief or sadness that overcame me. It was the opposite. It was my entire life feeling silenced, fighting against invisibility and attempted erasure. It was a dam or a dike bursting open somewhere deep in me and generations of water rushing out.

> *Tulips and daffodils fill with golden light*
> *mark this valley in never-ending fight*
> *a never-ending fight*

violet yellow red
cover tidelands
a settler's lot
remind me what used to be
invasive blossoms bled
farmlands for the dead
forgotten crops
remind me what used to be
Bury! Bury! Abundance once was
Carry! Carry! Our canoes away
across farm flats a valley
engulfed in flames
violet yellow red
cover tidelands
a settler's lot
remind me what used to be
petals settle everything
an ocean of color
of water we dream
dikes and ditches to change our land
chapels in branches
old ways banned
your bells our doom
your bells erasure in bloom

Basket Woman

※

I saw a red dress hanging from the branches of a cedar tree near my home in Tacoma, Washington. It moved in the breeze like a ghost, like it was dancing. It was an eerie sight, something that spooked me to the point of stillness. I watched it sway side to side. I imagined the body that once filled the fabric, could see her standing in the shadowy corner of a dimly lit gymnasium, at a school dance, lonely and waiting for a partner that would never come. I saw her walking along Portland Avenue in the rain, something I've done many times, the wet pavement reflecting the neon sign of the Puyallup Tribal Casino. I could not look at the dress without imagining the body's last movements, her final story, whoever she was.

Red dresses get hung up around tribal communities to honor missing and murdered indigenous women. Our sisters, mothers, and daughters who are lost and not found don't get lengthy news stories or headlines. We get empty fabric in shades of red. It's hard not to want more, not to demand national attention. When I remember the dress hanging in the tree, I see my niece's face. She's twelve, and once after a night of junk food and cartoons I drove her home across the reservation, just around the corner to my sister's place. I dropped her off in the parking lot and watched her take the steps up to her apartment, two at a time beneath the flickering streetlight. I pulled away but before I made it home, she called me. "Auntie, the door is locked. I can't get in." I hadn't waited long enough. My heart fell into my stomach, and my face flushed with panic and tears. I whipped around in the middle of the road, angry at how stupid I had been, how I had left a child I loved alone in the night. I sped all the way back and found her on the curb and took her home, apologizing the whole way. The fear lingered as I lay awake in my bed, long after my niece was asleep in the guest room. It was all-consuming. I began to wonder if it was the place that generated the anxiety. This is the Eastside of Tacoma. This is the reservation. We are close to the casino, close to the interstate. Would I have felt the same way if we were tucked into the brightly lit, manicured lawns of a wealthy Seattle suburb? Would I have lost my breath the same way if my niece had been locked out of a large house, in a gated community, where every house had an alarm system? But that isn't our reality. Safety is something we have to work for. I went to bed plagued by fear and guilt. I dreamt that night of a tribal legend, one I could recite from memory. In my dream I was chasing my niece through our dark neighborhood. But as I ran after her, stretching my hands out, she was always just out of reach. That's when I noticed something was behind me. I heard heavy footsteps, smelled sap and fire smoke. I turned to face the thing that was stalking me but woke just before she came into view.

My great-grandmother told us stories by the fire. They always began this way: *Ɂal tudiɁ tuhaɁkʷ. A long time ago.* The first time I heard the Basket Ogress story I was young. We were camping out at my great-grandparents' beach property on the peninsula. I remember the sword ferns casting shadows on our faces as we sat next to the crackling flames. We sat on split logs and damp earth. The trees towered in the distance. Beyond our circle, a ladder to the beach, then the sound of waves crashing. Around the fire it was warm, a family bathed in amber light and the smell of burning cedar. But if you stepped outside of the circle, it was only shadows and branches, trees bending and creaking. The darkness had a sound.

I was too young for horror movies and R ratings when I first learned of Basket Ogress, and she scared me more than anything I had seen on a screen. *Ɂal tudiɁ tuhaɁkʷ. A long time ago, there was a Basket Woman.* Sometimes her basket was woven out of cedar. Sometimes it was made of snakes. It differed depending on the storyteller. Her basket was the constant, always big enough to snatch up small children and carry them off into the darkness. Basket Ogress could make children disappear. The versions of the story would

change. Sometimes the children outsmarted the
woman. Sometimes they were able to get away, but
the details of the kidnapping were what stuck with us.
My sister and I would huddle close together in our tent
long after the adults went to bed, too scared to brave
the darkness and the trail to the outhouse. We'd ignore our bladders until we couldn't take it. We'd hold
hands the whole way, and when one of us was in the
outhouse the other would stand watch, shivering and
staring at the bit of trembling light coming through
the carved moon in the wooden door. What was more
frightening than each snapping twig or rustling fern
was that we knew she was coming. We were so sure
she was out there, waiting for us. Each time Grandma
told this story she'd insist that if you don't misbehave,
if you mind your elders and don't wander too far,
you'd be safe from Basket Ogress. But even at a young
age I questioned my goodness. I'd stand perfectly still
outside as my sister hurried in the toilet, convinced I'd
be the one taken, because I was the bad one. I never
said it out loud, but it was as certain as anything.

It wouldn't be long after those trips to the peninsula that I'd come to fear new things. In the place of
Basket Ogress were gore-filled horror movies, then
worse, predators out in broad daylight. Men who cat-
called and whistled at my changing body. At twelve
my body became a body overnight, and even though I
tried to hide the hips and curves of my new form, it was
like they could see through my disguise to the woman

beneath. Once, in the seventh grade at a crowded park with my family, I became acutely aware of a grown man staring at me. I went to the bathroom and when I came out he was there, close and smiling. It was brief, maybe only seconds, but something about his menacing smile, his yellow teeth and his eyes on my body, terrified me more than anything. My heart raced in my chest and not even the crowds and the sunshine could make me feel safe. I didn't tell my mother or any of my siblings, but something about him scared me so badly I ran all the way to the car. I sat alone. It was ninety degrees out, and as my brothers and sister played, I hid with the doors locked, waiting and sweating in the heat. Again, it was like I knew something about me that no one else did, something between that man and me, and I was too ashamed to admit it out loud. So I submitted to it, to the fact that I was maybe a bad one, one that could easily go missing.

Fear mixed with loneliness is a dangerous recipe. When I look back on it, I can't help but feel sadness for my adolescent self, for all the girls who ever felt for one second that it was their body's fault that men were being creepy. I shudder when I think of the girls who might have done what I did, who just embraced the fact that they could go missing. I think of all the systems put in place to reinforce this certainty. They serve as reminders, to make sure we don't forget we are disposable.

Recently I was interviewed for a sexual violence prevention podcast. My friend asked me questions about my experience, what it was like to tell my story, and then asked me if there was anything I'd like to see different in the world of sexual violence prevention. I thought about this for a long while before answering. I remembered my child self, faced with the task of talking to the FBI. When kids are hurt in movies and television series, there are cups of cocoa and blankets. The kids on TV are treated with care, given a lot of support. It wasn't like that on the reservation. "I want communities like mine, like the reservation I grew up on, to receive more care, or more attention, around these things." Because certain communities require more—specifically tribal communities who have endured generations of violence, historical trauma, settler colonial trauma, and the wounds that come with attempted erasure. It began to occur to me that questioning my self-worth, my own goodness, and the history of Native people were somehow linked. I considered the violence put upon our communities, the fear that overwhelmed me the night I drove away from my niece too soon, the red dresses hanging in the branches—all of it was connected.

The thing about our stories is that they haven't been told. I grew up with movies and narratives that constantly promised me rescue. If you're a girl who's been taken, your CIA father is Liam Neeson and he will find you. Or search parties and helicopters will be deployed, and no one will rest until you are found. It's easy to forget that you matter less; when you're only seeing things through a white lens, through pop culture and movies, it's skewed. It's search parties and flashlights, it's whole neighborhoods covering unimaginable amounts of ground until little whoever is found. But as an adult I've come to realize that isn't the reality. At least not mine.

In the United States, indigenous women are murdered at a rate ten times higher than other ethnicities. More than four out of five indigenous women have experienced violence. I first heard the words *missing and murdered indigenous women* when a friend explained a rally she was attending. As she shared the statistics of the rates at which Native women go missing, I was troubled by how immediately it all made sense to me. It felt obvious in a way that I hated. It's hard to describe how this information felt hardwired, something innate, a history that is just too familiar. I imagined my younger self, back in front of that outhouse, how easily I had accepted my fate that I might just be taken.

I take my story; I pick it up and move it. I drop it right in the center of a white cul-de-sac, with manicured lawns and prize-winning roses. I imagine us there with all the wealth and the privilege that come with places like that, things like PTA meetings, birthday parties, and iced tea. That is a different story. That's bloodhounds and search parties. If what happened to us happened in a wealthy neighborhood, the people who lived there would have time to let it sink in. I imagine that the men who hurt children, who hurt women, who hurt anybody really, are chased down by an angry mob, driven out, or at least forced to face justice, to pay for their crimes. But when these things happen in communities that are already struggling simply to survive, who has time for pitchforks and court hearings?

The news has a way of yanking me out of my fantasies. It reminds me that no one will look for us. It tells us we don't matter. Years of colonization and white supremacy have already laid the groundwork. When the first settlers arrived here, they were righteous, puritanical, and god fearing. There are accounts of indigenous women who disappeared, vanished from the census reports during the time of the fur trading routes. Indigenous women were viewed as something less than, their brown bodies were exotified, seen as dirty, capable of vanishing. The idea that Native bodies are disposable has been carried through the generations and validated through the white lens of the media. When a young woman, a white hiker, went missing, the story was everywhere and images of her flooded the news. Her face was on every screen. I remember her big smile, loose floating golden curls, some unknown landscape blurred in the background. But as the days went by and more and more images of her face were projected from every outlet, I started getting angry. Because it looks different when you go missing in indigenous communities.

When I was young my parents told us a story. Someone had abducted our cousin. I remember wanting to cover my ears, to shut out the details, like closing your eyes during the scariest parts of a horror movie. She was older than us but only by a little. She was babysitting her younger siblings. She had fallen asleep on the couch with the TV on. A man had been watching the house. He waited until her parents left for their night shifts and let himself in through the sliding glass door. For years I was too afraid to ever sleep in a house with a door like that. I imagined him stepping gently over the toys, familiar things, piles of laundry. While the house was sleeping, a stranger wrapped my cousin up in the blanket she slept in and threw her in the back of his truck. He drove away with her; it was that easy.

My cousin woke up in the woods after he left her there. She ran through the trees until she found a house and someone who would help her. My parents told us she was lucky to be alive. And I hate that because it's true, because the story would haunt me for years afterward. Like our tribe's story of Basket Ogress, it stayed with me. Our hearts raced every time Grandma told this story. We'd gasp and squeeze our eyes closed tight against the night, afraid of the shadows in the trees. We'd hold our breath at the scariest parts, like when she'd cake sap into the children's eyes so they couldn't see. Our hearts pounding as we lay awake. I can remember the feeling of my sister's hand in mine, the sound of the waves on the beach. The dark was terrifying because we believed something was out there, could grab us at any moment. So after my parents told me what happened to my cousin, I was angry. I couldn't stop thinking about Basket Ogress. Because this new story broke the rules. In this reality it didn't matter if you minded your elders or stayed close to the village, because this boogeyman could walk right into your home, could snatch you out of your own living room.

On a camping trip in my thirties, I drove out on the old Skagit Highway in a truck full of friends. As the road hooked and curled along the river I looked out at the dense woods and the abandoned buildings. The car ride became a tour of my teenage memories. *There!* I'd point, half laughing, at an old warehouse and recall nights spent drinking whiskey. I remembered hitchhiking and going to generator shows in the middle of nowhere. Or the abandoned house a friend and I got stranded in for two days. I said it lightly, but when I looked around at the faces of friends in that truck no one else was laughing. And suddenly I felt foolish for joking. I felt the weight of it, of what was at stake back then. Because I know now that I had been one of the lucky ones.

To look back from a distance, I can see through the toughness, the facade of bravery. I slept in skate parks, at truck stops, feigned fearlessness at parties. But I was always pretending, trying to cope by masking. I am full of fear when I think of my niece. I hate thinking of her ever in danger, or hitchhiking, or being out late, or her mother not knowing where she is for even one second. It's easy to dismiss my own precarious safety, but not hers. This of course makes some sense to me, to value someone else's life, especially someone young and innocent, over your own—but what gets me is the worry that there are entire generations of indigenous women who don't deem themselves worthy of safety. And how could we? When we're constantly reminded that there won't be search parties or torches, or hounds on leashes sent out into the dark to find our bodies? I look at my niece. At twelve years old she's sweet, silly, and curious about things. She likes to draw and tells me about the books she's reading. Already the odds are stacking up against her, against her indigenous body, her brown skin, the fact that we live on a reservation. There are systems in place that still wish to erase her—like the country that obsessed over the white hiker who went missing, this blond teenager, rattled by her disappearance. But when one of us goes missing, we don't get the front page or the five o'clock news. We get red dresses. I walk around my neighborhood in Tacoma and I still see them hanging. They serve as a reminder of the indigenous girls, the brown bodies that are still missing. I see the dresses swaying in branches, hanging from signs, and it's hard not to feel angry that they're even necessary. Why does a white hiker get every channel, her face filling up so many screens, and this is what we get, a red dress hanging, empty, like it's already become a ghost? I want my niece to know she's worth more than a dress waving in the breeze. I never want her to question that the whole world would stop if she ever went missing.

So I go back to our Basket Ogress story. How it frightened us is maybe the best part about it, because it was meant to be a warning. Our great-grandmother was trying to teach us something. And as I've grown older, I don't see Basket Ogress as the monster she once was. I choose to see her as a protector. It was a story meant to keep us safe. I think of Basket Ogress when I attend rallies for missing and murdered indigenous women. She's in the speeches and the songs. And maybe the story shifts and changes with the generations. It isn't enough to simply tell us to stay close to the village anymore, but we must remind ourselves that we are worthy of search parties and safety. And things are perhaps changing. Like the red dresses, the marches, the signs that read NO MORE STOLEN SISTERS; there are people singing and protesting. They are demanding the world start paying attention. And like in our own stories, it's up to us. If the news won't cover our abductions, our deaths, and our vanishings, if they won't plaster our faces all over the screen, it's up to us to keep from disappearing.

ʔal tudiʔ tuhaʔkʷ. A long time ago there was a Basket Woman. And I am grateful for the story, for the words our grandmothers chose, for knowing that the fear of going missing might actually teach us something.

Bəsxʷuqid

※

Swan Creek

When I first arrived in Tacoma, my life resembled a project abandoned mid-build. There were bones, a structure, the scaffolding that held me together. But there were holes. Holes in my memory, my heart, and my womb. I arrived unfinished. Half-done. I arrived in the middle of something.

My new home was a mess of boxes, a maze of empty rooms I had intended to fill with a body that never came. I bought the house out of necessity, a form of survival. I had been pregnant and living in a Seattle friend's bedroom. It seemed like the right thing to do. I needed a place to land. A place to make a home. I had always cared little about the stability of my living situation until I found that my body was hosting another. She had made a temporary home in me, and I knew I needed to give her another, more permanent one. One with walls and warmth, something that would last.

The word *miscarry* still bothers me. It suggests the mother-to-be has done something wrong, has made some mistake along the way. I couldn't separate the *mis-* from my body. *Misstepped, misspoke,* like my womb had *misunderstood* the assignment. If you look up the word *miscarry,* you'll find the second definition to be "an unsuccessful outcome of something planned."

Unable to bear the emptiness of home after that, I took to walking. A lot. I live on the Puyallup reservation, and just around the corner from my house is a park known locally as Swan Creek. My dog is a desert dog. I adopted her in New Mexico while attending school and she's never quite accepted the rain. Still, she dutifully trotted alongside me on my many walks. I think she knew she was doing me a favor. In drizzles and in downpours we explored Swan Creek.

The park stretches over almost fifty acres of land, the site for a new housing project in the 1940s. The plans fell through and the project was abandoned. An unsuccessful outcome. There are empty lots and moss-covered sidewalks. City blocks that go to nowhere. In the gray morning a thick fog blankets the park and it's like walking through a postapocalyptic dream.

It was perfect.

I was drawn to its emptiness. The quiet stillness of a place that was started but never finished. While my dog chased squirrels and chipmunks up the trunks of old-growth trees, I hovered over a sidewalk drain, drawn by its useless beauty. Perfectly intact but serving no purpose. I saw sewer covers in the pavement, cracked sidewalks designed to lead to homes that would never be built. I saw a broken and abandoned place. I saw my own body and felt less alone in it. There was beauty in the way nature had begun to reclaim the space, in the way the green and the wet earth swallowed up the concrete. On walks I'd wonder how long it might take for a full erasure. How many years until there was no evidence of humans having been there at all?

Walking with my dog along the cross-hatched roads, passing empty lot after empty lot, I couldn't help but wonder, what mistakes had they made? What was here before?

According to the park's website, Swan Creek once served as temporary housing for war workers. In 1941 thousands of military personnel flooded Tacoma, and temporary homes were constructed only to be demolished at the end of the war. There had been plans for a landfill and for a multiuse park, but the federal government eventually proposed a low-income housing project in the area named Salishan, in honor of the land's original inhabitants.

The park gets its name from the creek that runs through it at the bottom of a deep ravine. My dog and I often walk the steep switchbacks down to the creek bed. The Puyallup tribe once used this land to fish the salmon-bearing waters. There is an abundance of salal and salmonberry. In the trees you can still see where the bark had been harvested for weaving.

According to the Metro Parks website, when the reservation system ended in 1886, the tribal land was divided up among Puyallup tribal members, including a stretch of land along the creek belonging to John Swan. John Swan is listed in the 1887 census records as an "Indian Half Breed." He and his young wife had not received a formal education, yet according to the document were "trying to assimilate into white culture." John Swan, the Indian half-breed who once resided along the creek that bears his name, eventually sold the majority of his parcel.

The land changed hands. The city's attempts at development fell flat, and for years Swan Creek was left abandoned.

When I first arrived in Tacoma I was still healing from the miscarriage. I bled onto phone-book-thick pads and curled myself against hot water bottles and heating pads on the couch. My body fought to repair itself in the aftermath of what had happened: a simultaneous birth and death, an unsuccessful outcome of something planned. The doctors told me not to worry. That they believed a successful pregnancy was possible for me. My ex-husband told me he would try again, that if I wanted to we could try again. I wanted to. I closed my eyes at the crossroads in my mind. One path led to something expected, something I had craved most of my life, a home, something stable. I wanted to invent something that I had never had: safety. I wanted the chance to be the kind of mother I knew I could be. Down the other path was a dark unknown. When I tried to envision what lay ahead, I found only the shadowy and ominous road of a childhood fairy tale. A path thick with leaves swirling and branches that twisted and curled like hands, the road you never want your hero to venture down but the one they inevitably choose. So I told my ex I couldn't do it. Some deeper desire to be better, to heal, drove me into those dark woods. I tried to explain to him that I loved us too much to do that to us. Because more than I craved stability, or some fantasy of family, I yearned to feel whole. Perhaps it was never about motherhood to begin with. I began to think of my life beyond the conventional fairy tale, beyond the "he and I" story I had spun. Being whole had more to do with wounds that needed healing than with creating something new.

It was hard to look at anything new scattered around my empty home. The things I possessed were stacked in boxes that I didn't have the energy to unpack. What was there was half a life. Two wine glasses out of a set of four. Half a collection of old DVDs. Two crates of records where there used to be entire shelves full. I tried not to measure my life by the things I had lost. So I spent time outside. I walked in Swan Creek.

Beyond Swan Creek's sprawling expanse of abandoned streets and dead ends, I found trails that laced through wooded areas and lost myself on them for hours. I preferred the canopy of trees to my own roof. My love of staying outdoors even forced me to purchase something I never thought I would own: a grown-up raincoat. Eventually I began to take friends to Swan Creek, excited to show them this abandoned place, a place that felt to me like a ghost story, one that was comforting. Their reactions varied. One friend complained the entire way about the steep switchbacks. When we arrived at the creek in the peak of summer she moaned, *That's it?* I looked at the unimpressive trickle of water flowing before us and smiled. *That's it,* I said. I brought a date on a rainy morning and we laughed at a brightly colored child's plastic toy busted apart and draped over a tree. *It's an art installation,* she said, and for months afterward, if we'd happen to text, she'd ask if I'd seen any new installations.

Do you even want kids? one friend asked as we walked along the creek on a wet afternoon. We had been talking about my recovering body, my home as it began to take shape. I shrugged at her question, because the truth was that I didn't know. My wanting to be a mother was born out of a need for belonging. It was site specific. I had wanted to

belong to someone, or for someone to belong to
me. It came from some part of me that I had abandoned. *I mean, look at your life*, my friend continued
as we made our way back up the switchbacks and
toward the paved streets. *It's pretty amazing.* It was
true. I had been adjusting to life in Tacoma. I had
joined a band, gone on tour, taken trips to see a new
love in Southern California. I spent Christmas on
a beach and went swimming on New Year's. My
home began to fill with friends and artists instead
of children. It was full of a family of a different
kind. Back on the streets of Swan Creek that led to
nowhere, I hovered over a drain, its moss-covered
metal grate. I thought of broken things. Abandoned things. But I thought of the vines climbing
up the pavement. I thought of curbs and sidewalks
blanketed in green, in new growth.

Someone told me I should consider children more
seriously, that if I didn't make up my mind soon, time
would run out. *Women have a window,* she said, *and
when it's closed, it's closed.* A month later I was boarding a flight to Hawai'i to spend a month writing in
South Kona. I was visiting my partner's family on
the Big Island, and as I looked out the small oval window to the turquoise ocean below, the lush green and
the volcanic rock in the distance, I wasn't concerned
about timelines or windows closing. As I stepped out
into the fragrant heat, all flowers and Kona coffee,
my partner greeted me, eager to show me all of his

favorite places from childhood. I knew then I was exactly where I wanted to be.

There was a moment in my life that I spent planning to be a mother. I took prenatal vitamins and read books on pregnancy. I even bought that house. I worked hard to create the space I knew a child would need, a room with four walls, a window, a roof. Some animalistic instinct to build a shelter pushed me every step of the way. When I miscarried, I was angry at the emptiness of the large house I no longer needed. I saw a wasted nest. I saw an unsuccessful outcome of something planned. But as I began to unpack the boxes and hang the paintings, as I planted things in my garden, I realized that I had what I'd always wanted: a place that was mine, a safe home. I try to imagine a different outcome. I often wonder if I would have ever cemented something as concrete as a home for myself without the primal instinct pushing me to do so. If I am honest with myself, the answer is no.

I have never felt the pull to be a mother again. Some women are wired differently. There is no child-shaped hole in my life. There was grief, there was loss, but there is nothing missing. The place in my body that once felt empty, that grew grief deep and endless, is changing. Something like gratitude is rooting in me. My body knew something deeper before it ever loosened and broke the thing that had been planned. It pushed me every step of the way and when it realized we'd made it, we'd arrived someplace safe, it let go.

At home I stay up late writing. I sleep in when I need to. I leave for weeks at a time to join the person I love on wild adventures. Sometimes I watch my niece. I let her sleep over. I let her play video games far later than I should. We make popcorn and eat cake for dinner. Then in the morning I take her home to her mother. She's always smiling when she says, *See you next time, Auntie.*

Now when I think of my friend and her question— *Do you even want kids?*—and her timeline for my body, I still shrug. The answer is *I don't think so,* or *Not right now.* And if that changes when it's *too late,* it won't be a tragedy. It'll just be a different plan. Like Swan Creek, my body was abandoned. And in that abandonment, it shifted and changed. It grew and bloomed and changed course.

The park is changing. The city is developing it. There are plans for dog parks and picnic areas. I found new landscaped trails weaving through the trees, and at first I was angry. I liked this place empty. But last summer as I walked the trails down to the water, I couldn't help but notice the sword ferns. I had never seen so many wilted and scorched by the record heat. And maybe it's naïve of me, maybe it's too grasping, but when I walked along the same trail and saw the same ferns, lush and green in the winter wetness, I hoped for a moment that maybe it was a good thing. If the park was changing, perhaps it meant that people were listening. Conservation projects, salmon habitat restoration, and volunteering—it's a start.

There was a time I walked in Swan Creek looking for ghosts, haunted by memory. To honor grief, one must first acknowledge loss. I used to walk the switchbacks all the way down to the water only to turn and walk back up and down again. I was never ready to go back to the house, to the home I'd created. So I walked the trails. I'd wonder what ever happened to John Swan, the park's namesake, the Indian half-breed, who according to the census and the website once owned the largest parcel of land before he abandoned it. I'd think of all that acreage over the years, empty and unused. John Swan and his wife are buried in the tribal cemetery just down the road from the entrance of the park. It feels important to acknowledge this.

Then one morning I turned back on the trail, finally ready to go home.

I still walk in Swan Creek, but like the park my body's changing. It's letting go of things. I no longer see myself in metal drains or crumbled pavement. I see myself in the pink petals of the salmonberry blossoms. I pick salal berries by the fistful in the summer and savor their dark sweetness on my tongue. I see myself in the new growth that sprouts forth and takes over something that has died.

Grief has a way of pausing things. It can momentarily bring your life to a halt. But in order to climb out, there must be a choice. The vines still swallow the pavement, the earth grows up around you, because the earth doesn't care about stillness or death.

A friend and I recently walked in Swan Creek together. They wandered the path looking at the bright colors of the blossoms. Spring seemed to be exploding around us in a rainbow of new plants and petals. *People never speak about the violence of this season*, my friend said as they cradled some delicate pink thing in their hand. *All this new life springing from death.*

Yəhaw'

The Creator has left the sky too low. We are going to have to do something about it, and how can we do that when we do not have a common language? . . . We can all learn one word, that is all we need. That word is yəhaw'—that means to proceed, to go forward, to do it.

— taqʷšəblu / *Vi Hilbert (Upper Skagit)*
in her telling of "Lifting the Sky"

n the winter of 2020, I drove to La Push with my partner. We wanted to stay next to the ocean for a weekend. We rented a cabin on the beach. We brought candles, board games, and rain gear. Of course, the Washington coast was dark and stormy in February, but our little cabin had a big bathtub and a fireplace. We watched the sky fall dark and heavy into the ocean. We enjoyed the storm from behind the glass of the big picture window and felt safe.

On our first morning in the cabin, we woke and made coffee. The storm had dissolved into a light drizzle overnight and we took the break in weather as an opportunity to explore the beach, the day already heavy with fog. We walked the length of First Beach, down to the rock wall of the jetty and climbed up onto the wet black stones. I pointed to the island in the distance and the tall trees enveloped in mist. *Elder Island.* This was a sacred place. Before the land was stolen and the settlers came to this coast, the Quileute people buried their dead high in the branches in burial canoes.

When we lost my great-grandmother in 2008, I didn't know what to do. I had fallen so deep into my own grief I worried I might never climb out. At night I closed my eyes and saw every memory I ever shared with her, and I slept. I slept for days and weeks. I tossed and turned beneath my blankets, buried in my mourning. I dreamt of waves crashing over me and whales swimming above me. When I couldn't take it anymore, the nightmares and the sea that became my bedroom each night, I drove here to La Push. I rented the same cabin on the water that we stayed in now. I unpacked my groceries and tried to write, but eventually I gave up and walked out into the rainy night. I remember standing at this jetty and crying out to the ocean. Like the water could somehow answer me. But all that came to me was the storm, those clouds, black and heavy.

My partner never got the chance to meet my great-grandmother, so as we made our way back to the cabin, I told him stories. I told him how I carried her name, our Skagit name, and how because of this, growing up, people would recognize me. *taqʷšəblu's namesake!* strangers would say excitedly, like I might somehow carry some of her in me. I told him about the tattoo I got the week she passed, the Lushootseed letters inked in bold red, spelling out our shared name. And about my trip out to this very beach, how I had grieved right here next to the waves. He asked me to tell him one of her stories. *I can't do that*, I explained, to his disappointment. My great-grandmother was a storyteller; it was her gift, not mine.

When my great-grandmother told our tribe's stories, she not only expected you to listen, but she expected you to participate. Her storytelling was active. It was alive and loud. It had a heartbeat. In her backyard in South Seattle facing the airfield, she held big gatherings. While the salmon baked on iron-wood stakes, my cousins and I played in the yard. We ran through the garden and slid down the hill on makeshift sleds our uncles had built out of cardboard. We picked berries and snuck grapes. We got grass stains. But when we heard the booming command of Grandma's voice, we came running. The backyard quieted. Even the planes overhead seemed to respect the oral tradition, and for the brief length of the story the planes flew elsewhere. We all listened.

Back inside the cabin, my partner and I listened as the rain hammered down on the roof. We began cooking. While looking up a recipe on our laptop, we saw news about the coronavirus. We read about its arrival here in Washington State. We exchanged nervous glances and opened another bottle of wine. That night after dinner we put on our parkas and ventured out onto the beach. Bundled up and full, we climbed onto the mountains of driftwood. *I love it here*, I said out loud, staring at the wall of waves that crashed down onto the beach like thunder. I made us a small fire and he asked again for a story. I relented and began by telling him of the time I dragged the boom box out to the beach, *right there*, I pointed to the sand ahead, *and I hit play*. After my great-grandmother died, I brought everything she had ever written and recorded out to this beach. Her stories looped in the night as I hit play and rewind, play and rewind, like I could conjure her back to me. I listened to "Wild Blackberries," "Loon & Deer," but mostly I listened to "Lifting the Sky."

When she told the legend of how we once lifted the sky and the world out of darkness, she told us how we had to work together. She directed and we followed. We grabbed our big poles. We learned one word. And when the time came to steady our poles against the fallen sky she'd say, *All together now!* She'd say, *Louder!* As a child this was my favorite part: seeing aunties and uncles, adults and children, their imagined poles in hand as we all shouted, *Yəhaw'!* The word would ignite in my small throat and burst into the air around me joyous and explosive.

But that night, as I sat alone on the beach with

my boom box, there was no one to shout with. There were no cousins or aunties, no poles in hand. Just me and the dark sky. My metal camping mug full of whiskey, the stack of tapes and CDs and the salt from the ocean. These things were my company. That's when my partner interrupted the story. *You were so lucky*, he said. He could see the tears brimming, he could see me falling into memory and grief. *Those memories are a gift. Those tapes, the recordings, they mean she's still with you.* And before we went inside, I held my phone close to the fire as it burned and crackled. I made a recording. For five minutes I held it there, getting the wood as it popped and hissed, the waves in the distance. I wanted to remember this moment.

The next morning, we drove into town for supplies. The news about rising COVID cases filled the car with a different kind of story, one full of fear and anxiety. *What's happening out there?* we both texted friends and family. We wondered if we should return home. I could see my partner was worried. But we had the cabin for one more night, and we had groceries. We went to Second Beach instead. We hiked the short distance through the old growth. We passed the small creek to the place the beach opens up into a gray expanse of sand and rock. I picked up a stick and traced my name in the sand. I watched as *taqʷšəblu* filled with water, then washed away.

Back at the cabin we played Scattergories and made hot soup. And though we occasionally scrolled through the news, I tried to pretend none of it was happening. Whatever it was, it could not reach us on this beach. My love asked again for a story. So I opened my laptop and patted the floor beside me. Together we sat by the fireplace and watched my great-grandmother on the screen as she told her story to an audience in the 1990s.

When our world began, the legend tells of a sky left too low. The people were lost in darkness. Sky people were entering the world below, and people were traveling into the forbidden sky world. People were unable to speak to one another because the creator had scattered the languages in every direction. When my great-grandmother tells this story, she asks her audience to go out into the woods. *Go, go*, she motions with her hands. "We're all going to need to find big sturdy branches. These will be our poles." The crowd, made up of children, students, and linguists, does this. We watched the screen as strangers lifted the sky. We watched them pretend. They laugh with her, lost in story.

A week after we returned to Tacoma, the government issued a stay-at-home order. Rather than fly back to San Diego, my partner decided to ride it out here, with me, in Tacoma. Together we learned how to buy groceries for a full month in one outing. We learned how to stay busy. We took turns taking care of each other when we had to. On the days the anxiety became too heavy for the other to carry, we'd assume the duty of comforting. Some days I'd try to write, only to find myself staring at an empty screen. My therapist asked me to remember my ancestors. He asked me to consider the old ways, when we lived collectively. *Think of the families all living in the longhouse. Think communally. Do you think even a basket weaver would be weaving when there is a mountain lion circling?*

So I put away stories. We learned to take walks, and we planted things. When the protests started happening in the city, we made our bodies useful. We went to the rallies with backpacks full of masks and hand sanitizer. During a rally held after the murder of Breonna Taylor, an indigenous activist introduced a young woman from the Tulalip Indian tribe. We listened to the story of her father being gunned down by police, on the reservation, close to his own home. At first she was shy and too quiet on the mic. Her voice trembled, wavering like her mouth had gone dry. I wanted to run to her, to put a hand on her back, bring her water, but as she spoke her voice grew louder, stronger. She told the crowd where she was from. *This is Coast Salish land!* the crowd shouted with her, supporting her. The crowd said her father's name.

She spoke about Coast Salish sovereignty, about solidarity with Black Lives Matter, about our fight against the same oppressor, the same colonizer. Hearing her voice as it went from quiet to strong, as she came into her power right there on the steps of the empty precinct, stirred something in me.

Another speaker shared the story he had been told by my great-grandmother. Watching him in the middle of the crowd of black organizers, white protesters, and strangers, I felt the word begin to rush into my throat. *All the people had to work together,* he said, *to lift the sky up where it belongs and get the world out of darkness. The people had to learn one word. And that word was* yəhawˀ*!* He made us yell it. And I found my voice because I had to, because my great-grandmother would have wanted me to. She would have made me yell it. Her stories were active, you had to participate.

During the weeks that followed, the sky began to change. Smoke from forest fires settled over the Pacific Northwest like a dark cloud. We had been in the house for days. We had cabin fever. One morning my love helped me secure my N95 mask over my face. Then he tied a bandana over it. *You need to get out of the house,* he said. My asthma made it dangerous to breathe the smoke-choked air, but he seemed to understand that being trapped was taking its own toll. As we walked along the waterfront, I felt a panic rising in me. The world, unrecognizable as it was, was terrifying. We talked about the rallies, we talked about defunding the police. We ran through the checklist of our loved ones, trying to take inventory of who was still healthy. As a Native woman, the word *pandemic* is particularly frightening for me. I am descended from survivors of the smallpox epidemic. I come from a history of attempted genocide by disease.

When it became too hard to breathe, my partner let me lean against him as we made our way slowly up the trail. By the time we reached the car, we found it blanketed in ash and I noticed for the first time how it fell around us like snowflakes. It was almost beautiful. Until I remembered what it was, until I remembered the fires and entire neighborhoods erased. I looked up at the apocalyptic sky, the red sun all science fiction and nightmare. I tried not to think of how it could get worse. I couldn't help but think about Cormac McCarthy's *The Road*. My partner had to gently nudge me out of my dystopian fantasy, and I looked at him over the hood of the car with tears in my eyes and nearly choking. *The sky is all wrong*, I told him. *The world is not the way it is supposed to be.* That's when he knew to take me home, to get a pot of cedar and rosemary boiling. My mother had instructed us over the phone how to use traditional medicines that would help me breathe.

A day later a strong wind came and cleared the skies long enough for us to crawl out onto the roof. I was still haunted by the images of it all: the rising cases, the police brutality. There was grief growing inside me, bigger than anything I'd ever known, and it started to break me. I was quiet for days at a time. I began to dream again of a storm over a sea. That's when my partner asked me to crawl onto my roof and sit with him. He asked me once more for a story. Outside on the roof I hugged my knees to my chest and sobbed. I looked out over Tacoma, the reservation, the casino frozen midway through construction, stopped by everything that was happening. I cried for the things we had lost, for the world as it seemed to be breaking. But it was his turn to take care of me, so my love pointed past the casino to the water beyond it. *Remember La Push?* he asked, his finger pointing out to the peninsula, toward the place we spent on the beach. *Tell me a story.* I remembered my phone, my recording. I pressed play, and the beach came back to me. Right here, on the rooftop, on a hot summer day. We listened to the fire crackling and the waves crashing. I closed my eyes and remembered my great-grandmother's face. I sucked in a breath and I told him, for the first time, our story.

In the beginning we were lost in darkness. We fought to understand each other as we hit our heads along the fallen sky. With so many different languages, we had to learn one word and that word was *yəhawʼ*. We went into the forest and found strong branches, sturdy sticks. We propped them up along the sky, and on the command of our shared word we worked together. We pushed, and we pushed, and we pushed. We pushed the sky up to where it belongs and lifted the world out of darkness . . . together.

SiʔaƛΊ: Orations: 3

※

*My words are like the stars that never change.**

When I was eleven, I longed for a change of scenery. I used to pretend I lived in Seattle. In my imagined life I worked at a magazine; I went to rock concerts. These fantasies took shape when I discovered that, just down the interstate, the city was flooded with bands and artists. In eighth grade, at a slumber party, I watched the movie *Singles* for the first time. The film only confirmed my belief that the city south of the reservation would one day be my salvation. But the city, like the movie, felt unattainable, far away. For a girl on the reservation, Seattle wasn't real but something for other people, something make-believe. But that didn't stop me from daydreaming, from hanging posters of bands on the particleboard walls of my bedroom. Posters of Nirvana and Soundgarden.

—

Soundgarden released a song in 1992, a cover of Black Sabbath's "Into the Void." On the Genius Annotation website, a description of the Soundgarden track reads, "The lyrics have been replaced with a speech by Chief Sealth (commonly known as Chief Seattle, for whom the city of Seattle was named), which happened to fit the meter of the song. The words promote an environmental movement." Soundgarden's lyrics speak of selling the land and the sky. They talk about the warmth of the land and the sparkle on the water. They added *Sealth* in parentheses at the end of the track title.

I've read through the version of Chief Seattle's speech provided by the Suquamish tribe's website over a dozen times. I don't find any of the lines from the Soundgarden song. The band was moved by his words but changed them. If the stars change, do the constellations remain the same? Is it enough that the sky is still there for us to try and find our way?

Reservation Riot Grrrl

Lay me spread eagle out on your hill yeah.
Then write a book about how I wanted to
die. It's hard to talk with your dick in my
mouth. I will try to scream in pain a little
nicer next time. White boy, don't laugh,
don't cry, just die.

— "White Boy," Bikini Kill

We didn't have riot grrrl on the reservation where I grew up. We didn't have venues or collectives or record stores. "Punk" was only something I saw in the movies or in passing. My parents would take us into the city and my siblings and I would look in awe at the teenagers gathered on a random street corner. Glittering in their studded vests and in a rainbow of spiked hair, they looked both dangerous and glamorous. Mostly they looked like their lives were far more exciting than the one offered on the rez.

The first time I heard Kathleen Hanna scream the lyrics to "White Boy," I was a teenager. I had already survived sexual assault. I had experienced firsthand the violence of my body being forced into something it wasn't ready for by a white boy who wouldn't hear me when I said no. So when I listened to her screech and howl into the mic, "I'm so sorry if I'm alienating some of you / Your whole fucking culture alienates me," I was hooked. I knew I wanted to be a part of this world, where girls could scream and yell and fight back. I knew I had found something that would hold me through my teenage years and help me survive.

But something was missing. It was missing anything that remotely spoke to my indigenous identity. Still, it appealed to me. It lit a fire in me that sent me chasing a world beyond the reservation, leading to my discovery of bands, and punk, and the DIY scene. It was a journey that lasted well into adulthood, until I finally found myself in a van with five other weirdos driving across the country, singing songs and performing spoken word about colonialism, sexual violence, and systemic oppression.

But the path that led me to the world I craved was so loud and so wild that I hadn't even noticed how white the way had been. It was blinding.

Outside of a rowdy punk venue in Chicago in 2018, my bandmates overheard two white women as they heatedly went over their plan to get us off the bill. *I mean, why would a band do something like this? It's 2018. They should know better.* My bandmates, who had retreated to the van to tune guitars and smoke cigarettes before the show began, were quiet as they

listened to the conversation. The women were un-
aware of the van, the open window, and my eaves-
dropping bandmates. *I mean, this isn't Coachella. WHY
does she think it's okay to wear . . . war paint like that? It's
so disrespectful . . . to, like, Native Americans.* I was inside,
hiding from the crowds of strangers in the cramped
bathroom and trying to ward off a panic attack. I
was going over my spoken word. I was practicing
my backup vocals. And I was wearing red paint, a
symbol of my lineage, of our Coast Salish longhouse
dancers. The women had seen me inside and decided
they would champion the honor of all Native people,
would come to the rescue, would get us canceled for
our cultural appropriation. Just before the women
stamped out their cigarettes and prepared to march
back into the venue to seek out the show booker, my
bandmate threw open the van's side door, coming
face-to-face with the two of them. *Not that it's any of
your business,* she said, *but our bandmate is Coast Salish.
And if you're curious as to why she's wearing paint on her
face, you can certainly ask her, not that she owes anyone an
explanation.* And one by one the band filed out, crush-
ing their own spent cigarettes on the pavement and
glaring at the two women who stood, finally, silent.

That's the problem with white punks. They've existed in an isolated scene of their own making, a scene
so exclusionary for so long, they don't even recognize
when an Indian is among them. When my bandmates
told me that we were almost "canceled" by a couple

of white girls who equated my performance with that of a Victoria's Secret model swaying down the runway in panties and a feathered headdress, I tried not to let it bother me. I tried to focus my energy instead on the love I felt from my band, the way they had my back, and the look on the two strangers' faces for the rest of the night, humiliation mixed with confusion. I could see the wheels turning, the questions. I didn't look how they thought a Native woman should look; I didn't fit the representations they had been fed. They had never seen a Coast Salish person before. As hard as I tried to shake it off, I left that venue in Chicago with a familiar feeling snaking through me, one that took me back to my first punk shows as a teenager outside the small town next to the reservation I grew up on. A feeling in my gut that screamed, even back then, even at fourteen, *This space isn't for you. This music, these bands, these white kids with their chains and their "Mohawks" are not for you. This is a white thing.* It was a lonely feeling, one that disappeared parts of my identity; still I kept coming back for it. I was drawn to this world despite its flaws.

The first time I heard Bikini Kill I still lived on the reservation. "White Boy" blasted through the speakers and exploded the world like a bomb. I hugged my knees to my chest, mesmerized, as I stared at the crappy little Sony boom box I had dragged into our small bathroom. My musical taste up until that point had been limited to what was available to me. I owned three cassettes: *The Best of Blondie*, *Madonna*, and *Janet Jackson*. I had a handful of CDs: Nirvana, the Cranberries, and *The Crow*'s motion picture soundtrack. When I discovered there was a college radio station that I could tune in to from the deeply wooded village where I lived, the musical desert I called home, it brought a new world to my doorstep. All the way through the trees, past the oil refinery and over the freeway, the Seattle scene blasted into my family's single-wide trailer. It came all the way from Olympia to the reservation. And it changed me.

I remember Kathleen Hanna's voice. That shrill, girl-like yelling that would shift into something dark and guttural ignited something in me. When the riot grrrl movement erupted onto the Olympia music scene, I was only ten years old. By the time I discovered it at fourteen, the riot grrrl scene had already begun to dissolve. But still I sought out any zines I could find, compilations and mixtapes from friends, anything that could bring this world closer to me. The thing about falling in love with a music scene from your reservation bathroom is that it's out of reach, left to interpretation. I remember tearing out pages from *Seventeen* magazine and *Sassy*; pictures of Courtney Love and Kurt Cobain and ads for hair dye and clothes that featured pretty white models with spiked blue hair and leather jackets replaced my unicorn posters and pictures of Egyptian pyramids. The music that poured in through those crappy speakers validated something in me, that I had grown up somehow, that I could leave this place, the reservation, and find something better. Kathleen Hanna sang about sexual abuse. Outside my counseling and group sessions at the tribal center, I had never heard someone talk about the things that I had experienced, let alone scream about them. Her songs made me feel less alone. They made me feel powerful and angry.

I fell in love with a group of women I had never met and with all the things I heard they did down in Olympia. I read about protests and groups of women that gathered to educate other women on safety, on self-defense. I thought about the things that had happened to me and for the first time felt angry that there had been no such movement in my small community in the woods. No one to pass me a zine that offered tips on getting home safely, on how to defend yourself against predators. Where were the reservation riot grrrls?

Still the music spoke to me. It gave me permission to talk about the things that had happened to me, and not just in group therapy or with my closest friends but publicly. By fifteen I had already made friends who played in bands, put on shows, made flyers, and put out their own demos. The first girl in a band I befriended was Shauna. She wore a leather jacket, played bass, and drove a Ford Falcon. The boys around me made me mixtapes stacked with Misfits, Adolescents, and Subhumans. But Shauna made me my first all-femme-fronted mixtape. She brought Bratmobile, L7, and 7 Year Bitch into my world. By the time I was sixteen we were close friends, and when she asked me to contribute to her zine I was thrilled. I wondered what I could possibly add to it. So I took the dirty magazines that a shitty boyfriend had given me on Valentine's Day and cut up the images of women's naked bodies. I reduced them to limbs and open mouths, to something unhuman, because that's how the gift had made me feel. Like my body wasn't my own, my desires were not my own, like my entire existence was for someone else, someone male. In the center of my collage, I wrote a poem about sex and control, about the male gaze and sexual violence.

The zine felt empowering, and I quickly fell in love with the art of text and image and with poetry and spoken word. The riot grrrl movement relied heavily on zines, on text and image, to get its points across, and I was inspired. One famous image I had come across was of a young woman in a miniskirt walking away from the camera. The caption read simply: *My short skirt is not an invitation to rape me.* All of a sudden, I felt I had the permission to embrace my hyperfemininity, to throw it in everyone's face and dare them to fuck with me. We were allowed to be strong, but we were also allowed to still be *girls*—that was part of it. It finally felt like I could embrace this dangerous part of my identity, my hyperfemininity, and harness its power.

I sought out more and more shows. I left the small town and the reservation to go to punk shows in Bellingham, Vancouver, and Seattle. Far away from the reservation I found a new home in basements and punk venues. I surrounded myself with bandmates and activists. We went to protests and anarchist bookstores. I felt for a time like I had overcome something, something that had to do specifically with my past, with my life on the reservation, a place where bad things happened. However, to simply abandon a problem, to erase it and walk away, isn't the same as solving it. And I had abandoned this core part of my identity, the part of me that grew up Coast Salish, the part that remembered the sounds of our traditional language. In its place I carved a new me. I cut my hair and bleached it yellow. I went home to visit my family less and less.

By my twenties I had moved into a large house in Seattle and filled it with friends, artists and musicians, and a partner whose band played weekly shows and toured Europe. Every weekend I was crammed into packed venues, dancing along to the music in a sea of sweaty bodies. But I began to notice that there was no one else like me, no one from the reservation just an hour north on the interstate. I began to wonder where the Native punks were, if they even existed. This became so glaringly obvious to me week after week that once I even found myself staring at a stranger from across the dimly lit DIY all-ages venue. He walked in and I immediately clocked him. *That guy has got to be Native*, I said to a friend. *Who is he?* The stranger was a local musician in the scene, and though I never spoke to him I noticed every time he was in the room. That's a strange brand of lonely. *Another Indian*, and I'd keep myself from staring too hard, trying to imagine what tribe he might be from. Years later I'd remember his face as I sat in the fluorescent waiting room of Indian Health Service for some routine checkup. As I sat amid the elders and the single mothers, there he was, waiting with the rest of us. I smiled as my name was called and thought to myself, *I fucking knew it.*

The punk scene of my twenties in Seattle was so white that I let it eclipse me for a time. Until the loneliness got to be too much. Until moments in which a white singer wearing feathers and face paint would push me to lean in close and ask the friend next to me, *Is that person Native?* When the answer was no, the friend next to me, white, would shrug and abandon me in my discomfort. *But . . .* I'd start to argue, only to be drowned out by the wailing of guitars and the "This next one is called . . ." I would shrink myself into something quiet, but a rage was beginning to simmer deep in my guts. Mostly I was lonely. I craved conversations that allowed the space for topics like cultural appropriation, generational trauma, and attempted genocide. The punk scene was a place to air your grievances loud and angry into the mic. But no one was angry about the same things I was. It wasn't enough anymore to yell and scream, fists in the air, about only the police, about late-stage capitalism and corporations, sexism, and oppression. What about the rest of it? I'd try to engage in conversations at after parties and occasionally find an enthusiastic anarchist, some dude who had read *Bury My Heart at Wounded Knee*, and for a moment the two of us would find some common ground.

If you want to see more Native punk bands, a friend said to me once, *why not just start one of your own?* It seemed the most obvious solution but far harder to execute when the scene is driven mostly by white men. My ex-husband often dangled the idea before me, only to rip it away again. *We can't be in a band together*, he'd explain, *it's too messy.* I'd be left to wonder: Too messy because I'd be bad at it? Or too messy because I'm your wife? Or too messy because I'm a woman? So for years I took a back seat. I played roadie and merch girl. I'd sell T-shirts on tour and cook food for bands that stayed with us. Like the loneliness that rooted in me at mostly white shows, I felt a similar silence begin to take root in me. *You can be my wife, but you can't be in my band. You can be an Indian, but don't make it about being an Indian when some white punk wants to wear face paint and feathers. It's okay because they're singing about the plight of Native Americans. We're all fighting against the same oppressors. Besides, they've read* Bury My Heart at Wounded Knee, *it's cool.* Eventually this idea that I was a punk first and a Native person second became unbearable.

By the time Medusa Stare approached me at a party to ask if I'd join their band, I was ready. I was tired of being quiet. I wanted the chance to take the stage with a group of punks who actually wanted to make space for indigeneity. Onstage I wore red paint, my family's symbol of healing. This was personal; it was something sacred, something I had to ask permission for. When the white ladies in Chicago wanted to get us off the bill, I suppose their hearts may have been in the right place. They were just ignorant. When white punks steal tribal imagery, wear regalia and face paint, it's offensive and I'm happy to see appropriation no longer being tolerated. But what rattled me to my core was that these women just assumed I was not Native American. That's how invisible we've been in this punk scene. They had made up their minds about me and were so blindly dedicated to their white cause they failed to even consider asking me first, *Why are you wearing that?* To know that two white strangers outside of a punk venue were up in arms about the possibility of appropriation is a start, but it's not good enough. In their refusal to ask questions first, they did the very thing they were trying to prevent: they silenced a Native person and nearly erased my agency.

I think back to what first drew me into the punk scene. The idea of empowerment, of voice and agency, was the foundation of riot grrrl. And it inspired me. When I decided a couple of years ago to finally put together a Bikini Kill cover band for a Halloween show, I wanted to honor that empowerment and celebrate this thing that saved me at fourteen. Because on the reservation there were no protests or meetings, no zines for all the young girls who desperately needed an education in safety and self-defense. A month before the Halloween show, a friend was visiting and she asked me, *Don't you think it's problematic? To do a Bikini Kill set? It's just white feminist bullshit.* And I understood her critique. Riot grrrl was indeed a flawed movement, one that barely included BIPOC and trans voices. If riot grrrl happened today, I hope it would look different. I have faith that it would. But to discount the movement as something that did zero good wouldn't be true to my experience of it. Even as a kid out in the woods, in the cramped bathroom of a single-wide trailer on the reservation, it woke something in me, something that stayed with me. The years that followed I lived through the ways the punk scene failed people like me. I experienced isolation and silence and saw firsthand the exclusivity of whiteness in the punk scene. But like in any revolution, I think you can pick out the small victories and grow them like seeds. It's true, I wish I had seen something like riot grrrl take root in my reservation community, but some sliver of it found its way to me in that bathroom with that shitty boom box and it guided me. The liner notes of my old Bikini Kill albums and riot grrrl zines laid the foundation of what would become a writing career. Through them I found my way to poetry and performing. And I'm thankful for that.

The day of the Bikini Kill cover show I dressed like I had at fourteen: a plaid skirt, fishnets, and Dr. Martens boots. I wore a shirt I had scribbled on with a Sharpie, the words reading, I SAID NO. I went back to my teenagerhood, back to assault and date rape, back to toxic boyfriends, and back to the reservation, to the place I was both undone and remade.

In our set I jumped and screamed and howled. I sang the lyrics to "White Boy" like I was possessed by the younger me who so desperately needed to scream what had happened to her, to make sure people were listening. After our set, two young femmes approached me in the crowd. They smiled and hugged me, saying how happy they were to see *another Native person* singing in a band. They told me they were starting their own band, that they'd be singing about Native things. And that was enough for me.

Things are changing. When I was fourteen, it was all boys and all white and white-boy angry. Now there are indigenous queer bands, punk bands, goth and metal bands. I don't think riot grrrl got it completely right in the nineties, but I am thankful for the guidance it gave me, for the anger it sparked in me. It prompted me to question everything, to speak up, to fight back. And for two nights we played all the Bikini Kill songs that erupted something in me at fourteen. And for two nights I got to be something I had always wanted to see: a reservation riot grrrl.

Recently, I watched Bikini Kill play down the street from my home in Tacoma. I was thrilled to see the band playing a smaller venue, close to their place of origin, Olympia. As my partner and I stood toward the back of the crowd, I was convinced I'd be content watching the show from the outskirts. But when the music exploded into the showroom, I was overcome with a kind of bliss and adrenaline, that thrill of hearing a song that changed you played live, and it pulled me in close. My partner is over six feet tall and smiled at me as he waved me forward. He understood his place in a crowd that literally invented "girls to the front." So I inched my way through the crowd, ducking and weaving, smiling at the other showgoers. When I found an opening, I stopped and grinned at the stage, watching as Kathleen Hanna addressed the crowd. Just then a hand tapped me hard on the shoulder and I turned to face an angry white woman. She glared down at me as she shouted in my ear, "What the fuck is your problem, get the fuck out of my way." I jumped back and immediately apologized, taking one step to my right and out of her line of sight. She tapped me again. "Seriously," the woman wouldn't let it go and continued, so heated that she was flushed, "you think it's okay to just get in my way like that?" And I looked at her as I apologized a second time. The woman was about fifteen years my senior, tattooed, a blunt blond bob dyed pink in places. Everything about her screamed "I was there in the nineties." A real riot grrrl. The exchange was brief and uncomfortable. I stood through the next two songs on edge, feeling embarrassed. But as the band launched into their beloved anthem "Rebel Girl," there was nothing but joy erupting all around me. The crowd pulled and pushed me, yanking me away from the fuming woman and her rage. I moved with a wave of bodies toward the stage, all laughing and yelling and covered in sweat. And most of the audience members around me were not white.

After the set, I was steaming in sweat and euphoric, reunited with my partner and friends who hadn't rushed the stage as I had. Then I saw her, the angry white woman who had called me out in the center of the crowd. I thought about how she had screamed at me between songs, how everyone around us heard and offered sympathetic smiles in my direction, how embarrassed I had felt, how angry. Then I took a deep breath and put a smile on my face. I marched up to the woman and politely chimed,

"Hello. I'm so sorry I stood in front of you, I never meant to block your view, it was an accident." She offered a curt smile, arms crossed as she said, "Thank you." She nodded like I had atoned for some great offense, like royalty when they accept your apology and then make you kiss their jeweled hand. With the same giant grin on my face, I asked the woman for a land acknowledgment. "A what?" she immediately prickled. "What the hell is that?"

"Well," I explained in a saccharine, singsong voice, "I am a Coast Salish woman, a descendant of the people whose land this venue is on, whose land you seem to feel quite entitled to, and I'd just like you to acknowledge that, as a guest here." The woman, in her band tank top and her pink-and-yellow blunt bob, arms covered in tattoos and bracelets, looked like one of the people I might have seen in a magazine in the nineties, all the way back on the reservation, in my small room in a trailer in the woods, as I sat there making mixtapes like it was a ceremony. And maybe I would have torn the ad out and plastered it to my wall, because from way up there someone like her looked cool to me, like something I strived to become. The woman spat "Fuck you" right into my face, and I'm glad I found myself standing before her grinning as she nearly blew a fuse. I twirled around on my heels and danced my way back to my group and out of the venue, laughing triumphantly. Because maybe that woman will actually think about an indigenous punk girl telling her off, who asked her to consider something outside of her whiteness and her idea of what punk should be. Maybe she'll think about it all night, how she publicly shamed a Coast Salish girl on her own land, and maybe she'll feel bad and think. Or maybe not. But for a moment she had to face it, my Native anger, my Native land, my identity, a loud reservation riot grrrl.

The Jacket

※

As a young girl, I wanted the world of mermaids to be tangible, real, a world I could exist in. I learned to hold my breath underwater at the community pool, unafraid. This was especially difficult because I am an asthmatic; breath has always been a powerful and terrifying thing to me. The idea of drowning without water, of choking on nothing, of strangling simply because your body forgets a basic function, has haunted my nightmares since childhood. I have always wanted gills.

Mermaids, according to Hans Christian Andersen and Walt Disney, have always wanted something. They want it so desperately they will sacrifice anything to get it. Most often the thing is escape. They want legs. They want the ability to leave. They want a prince. They want anything other than what they've got.

I remember my first day of school after moving from the city to the reservation. When I stepped out into the dim, blue light of morning, it felt like something was wrong with my legs. I was nine years old, and this was my first time boarding the bus that would take me to La Conner Elementary School.

The move from city to woodland was frightening for various reasons. Mermaids, those half women, half fish, represent the ultimate half-breed, an obvious kind of duality that isn't muddy but is clear as day. A neighbor would never swim up, poke Ariel in the chest while eyeing the scales of her fin, and say, "Hmm, you don't *look* part fish."

There was no tribal school to attend on the Swinomish reservation; instead all the kids were shuttled across the channel to La Conner to attend the mostly white school. Here was a collision of worlds. Here was a pool of strictly fish and strictly non-fish, corralled together, and here I was, a pale person in a hand-me-down pink windbreaker. In my shabby floral-print leggings, oversize denim button-down, and Kmart-brand Keds knockoffs, I inched out. I looked back at our trailer, at my new home, as it stood against the trees. My parents' bedroom light glowed orange in the dark. I wanted to turn back. I studied my outfit as I crunched the gravel of our driveway beneath my sneakers. The only new things were the cheap, magenta knockoff Keds and the plastic barrette in the tangled mess of my brown curls. I inhaled shakily, my chest sputtering, and then exhaled. The shallow breathing always made me think of the time a classmate plucked the pet goldfish from its bowl and we stood in horror watching it gasp and thrash its tiny body against the linoleum until finally Mr. Hubert scooped it up and dunked it back into its home. I remember its eyes, puffed up and desperate, the slits of its gills twitching open and closed like two screaming mouths. The doctors at the tribal clinic would later inform my parents of my asthma, but this morning my stifled breathing was still a mystery.

I saw the yellow school bus streak through the cedar trees. I swallowed air and quickened my pace. Climbing up the big steps, I moved past the bus driver with her sunken face and stared at the columns of strangers. I felt fingers of panic close around my throat and reminded myself to breathe.

I saw Starter jackets. I saw shiny zippers cutting through the brightly colored sports logos. I saw jerseys on the kids from the rez, Polo shirts and name brands on the kids from La Conner. I felt in between something. I looked down again at my collage of hand-me-downs. I was neither sporty nor fashionable. I looked outdated. I shuffled to a seat and stared out at the wall of trees zooming by. Groups of kids huddled together, laughing at jokes I didn't understand. Whispering and sniggering came from faces brown and white and all unfamiliar. The only other Native kids I had been around were my cousins, brothers and sisters, our family's relatives. The only white kids I had been around were my peers at the inner-city elementary school I attended before my parents decided to move us up to the family's land in Swinomish.

"They're just curious about you," my mom would say each afternoon when I'd return home, complaining that no one had talked to me again. "They'll come around." My mother's observation felt accurate to me. I was new and from the city, and I let this strange sense of confidence root itself in me. I wore it like armor.

One afternoon, a girl in the third grade did get curious enough to finally approach me. Her name was Anna and she lived three stops ahead of mine on Indian Road. She usually sat in front of me on the afternoon bus rides home. I watched her golden head rest against the vinyl seat. It bobbed and bounced when she laughed with the gaggle of girls that surrounded her, and when she'd flip her blond locks over her shoulder, I smelled strawberries and sugar, a cloying aroma invented by shampoo commercials on television. She beamed around to face me unexpectedly one afternoon. "Hi!" she said brightly. "You're in Mrs. Middleton's class with me, right?"

I nodded, a little dumbfounded, a quiet, feral instinct tugging me further back into my seat. Unabashed, Anna launched into a barrage of questions and curiosities. She wanted to know what Seattle was like. She was confused when I shrugged at her question "But you're a white girl right?"

"No. I mean, yes. But I'm also Indian," I began, but she laughed and cut me off.

"So," she smiled, "you're only part Indian?" She moved right along and left me sitting on the roadside of that conversation. *Part Indian.* Like only half of me was bad. I shivered a little. Anna terrified me. She glowed with a kind of cleanliness I would never know, not even on the mornings after my family's weekly trips to Thousand Trails Campground. In those days, we didn't have running water on the property. The nights my brothers and sister and I enjoyed the luxury of hot water, shampoo, and soap always felt decadent. I'd go to bed those nights huffing my perfumed hair, feeling clean and proud, but there wasn't enough berry-scented Herbal Essences shampoo in the universe to make me as squeaky clean as Anna.

Before her stop came up Anna smiled, showing teeth. "You know, that first day you got on the bus, I kind of just thought you were some ugly girl. But you're nice." She flipped her hair, perfume strawberries splashed me in the face, and I watched her glide off the bus.

I decided to invest some time and energy into my appearance. Climbing up on the toilet to reach into my mom's makeup bag on the shelf was the first step. I wanted to transform, but I thought I'd better practice first. One Saturday morning, I spent the better part of an hour tugging my hair back into a scrunchie and applying my mom's makeup to my face. I wanted to look more like her. People always talked about how beautiful she was, so I figured I couldn't go wrong. I surfaced from the bathroom to the roaring laughter of my siblings. Even my parents chuckled. My mom's foundation was about three shades darker than my skin, and I looked like I had rubbed my face in dirt. I scrubbed my face back to its natural state and swore off makeup forever. I went back to my normal routine of life on Indian Road. I spent afternoons in the woods with my brothers and sister, hunting salamanders and poking around in the depths of decomposing logs.

Tara was my first real friend at school. I met her walking across the blacktop at recess one morning. I saw her first. Her brown hair fell to her shoulders; her eyes disappeared when she smiled a big smile. But what really caught me was her light-blue denim jacket, a perfect fit, not a hand-me-down. Its sleeves weren't rolled up into ridiculous cuffs around her wrists. There were no stains, no burn marks or holes, and the jacket fell right to the waist of her blue jeans. I had never seen a jacket so new. Most important, the back was adorned with a giant, sparkling decal of the Little Mermaid. Ariel. Painted in glittering colors, Ariel posed, her ruby hair floating in the sea of that jacket. I was immediately bewitched by the obvious sweetness of this girl and the perfection of her jacket. Tara exuded friendliness. I stood back, observing her. She jumped off the monkey bars and chatted with the girls around her. Then she walked right up to me.

"Hi!" Even her freckles sparkled. "What's your name? Do you wanna come to lunch with us?"

I must have looked like a wounded animal answering her questions. I was worried at each new inquiry that Tara's face would drop, but it never did, not even when I told her where I lived. Tara wasn't fazed by me living across the channel, on the rez. She kept chattering on, smiling and telling me about her mom's house out in the farm flats and her dad's house in town by the channel.

Right away, that jacket became an object of obsession for me. I coveted it so intensely I dreamt of strutting around school with it but would wake each morning to find it gone, the same pink thrift-shop windbreaker in its place. I begged my mother to take me to the mall, to the Disney Store, where I knew the jacket lived.

My mom would come home late after a long commute back from the Native group home where she worked. Exhausted, she'd ask us kids if we'd eaten, throw together a box of macaroni and cheese, and check on chores and homework. One night, she leaned against the sink, still in her work clothes—a burgundy pencil skirt and a white blouse—doing dishes. I paced around her excitedly. I described the jacket in all its detailed glory. I explained to her that Tara and I would have matching jackets! My mom put the last plastic bowl on the wooden dish rack. "Who is Tara?"

"Tara is my new friend," I beamed. "She lives in town!" My emphasis on *in town* caused my mother to look up from the dish towel she was patting her hands with. Her lips pursed the way they always did when she was irritated.

"In town, huh?"

"Yeah," I continued, moving away from what I knew my mom meant. *In town. Not on the reservation.* I circled back to the jacket.

My mom frowned. "We've already done the back-to-school shopping," she snapped, "and I don't know why you think money grows on trees, but we certainly can't afford to just buy all you kids fifty-dollar jackets. It's absurd! The one you have is perfectly fine. Enough about the stupid jacket!" She asked about my homework, looked at the clock, kissed me, and said goodnight.

The jacket was more than just status though. Ariel and I had a history. When I was six my mom had taken me to the Cineplex and bought me a Cherry Coke and a bucket of popcorn. This was a magical luxury—the neon lights, the smell of butter, the rainbow assortment of treats displayed behind glass. There was something extravagant about it, that first march down the dark theater aisle, holding an armload of candy boxes and sucking on the plastic straw of my soda cup. I felt rich. This is how kids on television went to the movies. The animated fairy tale exploded from the big screen in a world of color, singing fish, talking crabs, an evil sea witch, a handsome prince, and of course that iconic redheaded merprincess longing for a better lot in life. The Little Mermaid had a bunk deal, and I identified with that.

The ocean became my biggest fantasy. Ariel was hell-bent on trading in her fins for a pair of legs to walk on land, and I was her opposite. I longed to wake up one morning to find webbing between my toes, to slowly morph into a half fish and disappear beneath the surface. I knew I was just like that fiery and mischievous mermaid, only instead of escaping into a sea cavern full of treasures, I escaped into the forest behind our trailer. I built forts and talked to trees and daydreamed about leaving. That was always the Little Mermaid's deepest desire: leaving.

My mom catered to my mermaid fantasy when she could. We couldn't afford the jacket, so she tried to make up for that by throwing me a mermaid-themed birthday party. There, on the table, was a giant cake in the shape of Ariel. Her green tail, peachy torso, purple seashell bra, and crimson hair were all accurately portrayed in frosting and sprinkles. In the kitchen was a mess of pots and pans, different shapes my mom had used to sculpt and cut out my mermaid-shaped cake. I was horrified as we began sectioning her into chunks, carefully serving up squares of green fins, the belly button, a serving of purple seashell, her pink mouth. But as I watched my girlfriends around the table in their triangle party hats smile as streamers fell in purple and green ribbons beyond their heads and they enjoyed their personal portion of mermaid, I swelled with pride.

On ferry rides out to my great-grandparents' property on the peninsula, I squinted hard through the waves. I was determined to catch a glimpse of the shining scales of mermaid fins. During family camping trips out at the beach property, my great-grandmother and great-grandfather would get up at sunrise to take the ladder down the cliff to the ocean, where they would spend the morning digging for clams. I'd explore the beach's early morning tide pools while they watched for the squirt of geoducks in sand. I played out entire mermaid scenarios in my head as they filled their buckets with the clams we would eat for dinner. I'd carefully climb out over the rocks, squint at the horizon, and wish hard with all my tiny limbs that the merpeople that lived beyond the breakers would come back for me.

My great-grandmother was a storyteller, and I constantly tried to impress her. I would sit during the nighttime campfires perched on the edge of my stump as the fire cracked and lit her face in the dark. The lines in her brown skin were faint, and though she was past sixty, her cropped hair was a dense black, matching her eyes that glittered dark against the firelight, the cracks around them moving as she spoke. My great-grandmother told the stories in our traditional Coast Salish language, Lushootseed. I hung on each Lushootseed syllable eager to hear it repeated in English in order to make sense of the story. When she told stories, the whole family quieted to hear her words and the crackle of burning cedar. Desperate to impress her one afternoon, after a long morning of clamming and fishing, I sat down next to her as she cleaned and gutted a fish. I decided to test out my own skills as a storyteller. I sucked in a deep breath and launched into a play-by-play of Disney's *The Little Mermaid*. I left nothing out. I even sang the songs. I gave a brief history of where the fairy tale originated. My mother had taken me to the Seattle Public Library, and I had educated myself on all things mermaid. I knew it was based on Hans Christian Andersen's "The Little Mermaid," and I had seen the picture books and watched the animated film, discovering to my horror that the mermaid princess doesn't marry the prince in the original but tragically turns to sea foam at the end. My great-grandmother graciously listened. She smiled and nodded. She praised me when I was finally finished.

"You know," she said that afternoon at the beach, "your ancestors have their own sea princess." I nearly fell off my stump. I listened intently as my great-grandmother told me for the first time the story of the Maiden of Deception Pass.

The story tells of a maiden who lived with her people down by the water's edge. One morning, while gathering clams with her sisters, the maiden stepped into the ocean and felt it grip her. She heard a voice as the ocean spoke to her, reassuring her that he only wanted to look on her beauty. Each day she'd return to the beach to collect oysters and clams, and each day the ocean spoke to her. He beckoned her to come live with him; he pleaded for her to be his bride. One morning, the voice did not come, but a man emerged from the water, tall and handsome. He walked the girl through the village and asked her father for her hand in marriage. Her father refused, unwilling to part with his daughter and certain she would die in the ocean. The ocean left but warned the village that if the girl could not be his bride he'd bring on a drought. True to his word, the rivers dried up, and there were no clams or fish for the maiden's people to eat. The maiden's father finally refused to see his people go hungry and agreed to the marriage on the condition that his daughter be allowed to return to her village once a year, able to walk on land and be with her people. The ocean complied, and the two were married. In the sea, the maiden was happy. She was in love and enjoyed her new home but she knew her people missed her, and soon it was time to return home. Each year that the girl returned home, it became more difficult for her to walk on land. She returned each year covered in more bits of the sea. In the last year she returned, her father saw the barnacles on her face and the sea kelp that was her hair and heard the difficulty in her breath. He told his daughter he couldn't bear to see her in such discomfort and released the ocean from his promise to return the maiden to her people each year. The people of the village lived happily with their abundance from the ocean and knew that each time they saw the long streaming pieces of sea kelp floating in the narrow waterway of Deception Pass they were seeing their maiden's hair and she was still with them.

The Maiden of Deception Pass didn't just disappear into the ocean; she became the ocean. She sank into the sea to save her tribe from starvation. She returned each year like Persephone. But unlike Persephone, she went willingly into the depths, into the underworld. This somehow empowered her beyond the other sea maidens I had become so obsessed with. Mermaids were always bargaining with a sea witch to trade their fins for legs. Their motives were usually entirely selfish and almost always resulted in their demise. Selkies were a different kind of tragedy. Like mermaids, the half-seal women of Scottish folktales always sacrificed their life in the sea to be with human men, to be on land. The men often tricked the selkies, hiding their seal coats from them so they couldn't return to the sea. The selkies became depressed. They missed the ocean and their seal lives. They were captive. But unlike mermaids and selkies, the Maiden of Deception Pass wasn't a victim but a warrior, willingly braving the deep sea to save her people and find happiness. Selkies, mermaids, and even the Maiden of Deception Pass all got to go someplace else. They traded fins and seal coats. They left their homes.

I begged my great-grandmother to tell and re-tell the story as often as she would. I ran along the beaches with new enthusiasm and pride. The ocean and I were practically related. I hopped along the stony shores, ecstatic each time I'd see the rubbery shine of sea kelp on the surface. I'd scoop large bits of the maiden's hair up in my arms, happy with the proof of it. I felt connected to the water in a new way now.

Hearing the story of the Maiden of Deception Pass only intensified my mermaid obsession. Like I did with Ariel, I felt her in me. The only problem was that there were no Maiden of Deception Pass Barbie dolls or backpacks. I stuck with hoarding all the *Little Mermaid* objects I could get my hands on.

I had a *Little Mermaid* lunch pail, thermos, sleeping bag, and nightshirt and all the dolls available. Each birthday or Christmas brought a new Ariel artifact into my life, some new talisman that I could tote around. But the jacket was the next level. It wasn't some silly doll or nightie. This was fashion. This was grown-up and somehow sure to elevate my status from new girl who lives in a trailer, who isn't white but also isn't Indian, to Tara's new and popular best friend. Still, my mother refused. "We can't afford it." She said it so often that it began to sound as regular as breathing. Inhale: *We can't.* Exhale: *Afford it.*

One Sunday morning, my mom brought home a surprise. She had gone out for errands and returned with a giant bag from the craft store. She worked well into the evening, tracing and painting. By the time the sun had set, she called me into the kitchen to show me what she had made. She held up the Levi's jacket. It fit perfectly. If it was secondhand, you couldn't tell. And on the back was a near-flawless replication of Tara's Ariel decal. I burst into tears and laughter both. I jumped up and down. I quickly put the jacket on and tore it off again to admire the shimmering painting of Ariel. It looked like the real deal.

My mom pointed to the display of fabric paints strewn across the kitchen table, "Do you want to add something?" I nodded. She left the room as I scooted up to the table and picked out a pearly, seafoam green paint. I concentrated hard. I bit down and chewed my lip. I wanted my lines to be precise. When my mom came back into the kitchen I was sitting cross-legged in my chair, waiting for it to dry. "Oh," she smiled sympathetically, "It's L-I-T-T-L-E, dear." I looked down at my drying paint: *The Littel Mermaid* stared back at me, already drying in its pearly finish.

We scrubbed with wet towels and dish soap but the damage was done. *Littel* was still clearly visible through a cloud of pale green paint hovering above my mother's pristine replica. My mom reassured me it was fine, "No one will notice, honey. Your hair will cover it."

The jacket did look pretty good. I put it on the next morning and shook my hair over the collar. Maybe it did cover the horrible, puff-paint typo. I held my head high as I boarded the bus. I sat in my usual seat, kicked my legs back and forth, and hummed. I wore my jacket through first and second period. I wore it into the cafeteria at lunchtime. Sitting next to Tara, I ate my lunch and she smiled. "It looks so good," she said. "Your mom did such a good job."

Anna and a group of girls sat one table over, and as I sipped my milk through the small carton, as I bit into my PB&J on wheat, I began to feel their eyes burning into my denim back. "Oh my god," Anna squealed across the cafeteria. "Is that a hand-painted *Little Mermaid* jacket?" She had gotten up and was standing behind me now. I nodded, still holding on to the pride of my mother's fabric-paint masterpiece. I sat in the silent wake of what came next. I thought of the Little Mermaid and the Maiden of Deception Pass. I thought of sea kelp moving on water. The wave crashed. Anna's laughter was a shrill and stinging thing. "Well, whoever did it is *stupid*," she announced. "They spelled *little* wrong! You should take it back." She walked away, just like that day on the bus. Only this time there was no question. I was just some ugly girl. Worse. I was now just some stupid girl too. I trembled a little and stared at my plastic tray.

Tara smiled her sympathetic smile. "It's really not that noticeable. I think it looks nice." She tried to sound reassuring, but it had already happened. There I was, floating on the surface of the water, and not like the deep strands of kelp but broken apart, like sea foam.

I walked slowly down the gravel driveway toward our home that afternoon, the jacket a bundle of shame tucked under my arm. I pulled the metal door to our trailer open and bolted down the narrow hallway. I glanced at my mom, who sat chatting on the telephone before I slammed the door to my small room shut. I hurled the jacket into the closet and sobbed. I wouldn't ever wear it again. I heard my mother outside the thin walls of my room and sucked in a ragged breath.

The trailer started to shrink around me. Things felt smaller and I spent more time in the woods. I started pocketing my lunch money, skipping meals or shamefully sneaking the bland peanut butter and jelly sandwiches that were free in a large plastic crate next to the food line. I didn't dare remove the jacket from its crumpled pile. I shoved my saved-up lunch money between my box spring and my mattress, waiting until I had enough to go to the mall to buy something new to wear. I just wanted to look like everyone else. I'd go hungry. I'd ignore the rumbling in the pit of me. I'd come home and take off my pink windbreaker, open my closet and try not to look at it, the denim jacket in a pile in the corner of the small cupboard. If I looked too long I'd notice again the glittered lines, careful and precise. Ariel's face would appear, distorted in some fold of fabric, and I would see my mother, carefully bent over our folding table, patient and steady handed.

The Whale

✳

don't belong here, I used to say when I lived in Swinomish. Too half-breed, too full of wanderlust and dreams to be confined to the dense woods of my childhood home, I began at a young age to dream of leaving. I was going to be a musician, an artist, a writer. I was going to be anything other than a girl with dirt on her face and campfire smell in her hair. I didn't know how I was going to achieve my dream life of artist lofts and galleries in the city, but I knew Seattle was a good place to start.

Moving to the city made me miss my mother and great-grandmother. I went on long walks passing out résumés, and thinking of them I remembered the rustling of foil and fish at family gatherings. I closed my eyes and could see the plastic cups, the pink juice inside. I tuned out the sounds of traffic and could hear my great-grandmother's voice, the way she would hush the smallest of infants. "Hush!" she would say, "when grandmothers are speaking."

I started to listen to recordings of my great-grandmother's stories on a portable CD player. I rode the bus through the city and listened as she recited in English and Lushootseed. When the CD ended,

I'd hit replay. When my batteries died, I'd remember times around the campfire. I often recited the story of the Maiden of Deception Pass from memory. I'd think of the stories my great-grandmother told us about language work, about how she came to do her life's work in language revitalization. "Without language, there would be no culture," she said. I remembered those words. I heard them in my head each time I caught a glance of the gold-and-black cover of the *Lushootseed Dictionary*, the book she brought into the world. Without her, those words, our language, would no longer exist.

I had been in Seattle only a month when the whale showed up. As I sat in a coffee shop scanning the classifieds, this story caught my eye: "June 25, 2003. An adolescent gray whale visited the Skagit River in Northern Washington. The whale was spotted five miles inland near Conway." I considered the whale for a moment and wished I could be back home, standing on the bridge over the Skagit. It must have been a beautiful sight. I folded the classifieds and walked back to my new home, empty and still smelling of bleach and carpet cleaner.

Morning sun was not kind to the two-bedroom basement apartment. The white walls were spotted in faint yellow patterns—the phantoms of old cigarettes. The beige carpet was a Rorschach game of Twister:

left hand, forgotten vomit stain; right foot, old coffee spill. There were many boxes to be unpacked, but I ignored the ones marked BEDROOM, SHOES, and KITCHEN and instead ripped the tape from the small box labeled ALTAR. I carefully unwrapped ceramic candleholders, sprigs of cedar, stones collected from a riverbed in the Cascades, and a braid of sweet-grass. A small glass picture frame surfaced from the crumpled pages of the *Skagit Valley Herald*. Wiping the dust from its glass, I placed the photograph of my great-grandmother in between two bundles of cedar. It didn't take long to arrange. In the sparse beige apartment, the altar was a beacon. I lit the candles and pretended the little table was a mountain.

My basement apartment was next to the laundry room and the machines banged against my bedroom wall. The couple above me stomped and played their stereo through the night. The man across the hall had long, loud conversations with someone overseas, in a different language. I learned to love the noise. The trailer back home in Swinomish was a small and noisy space. I pretended the noises in the apartment were the sounds of family. The bangs and the clanks made me feel less alone.

I job-hunted. I called home twice a week. My mother's voice sounded far away, crackling through the cold black plastic of the pay phone. I asked how Grandma was doing and after that I asked about the whale. "Well," my mom said, staying caught up, "a reporter said that the gray whales like to follow food up there. Once they start, they may keep doing it. As long as they don't get stranded, there's nothing to worry about." I sipped coffee and tried to imagine the large belly of a whale in those shallow waters, scraping along the stones and sand, pushing its way through narrow channels, maneuvering around large river rocks and branches.

When I finally found a job, it was at a coffee stand inside the lobby of the Art Institute of Seattle. Every Monday through Friday, I woke up at 6:00 a.m. to make coffee for art students. I caught the bus when the neighborhood was still dark and opened the coffee stand as the sun came up. One afternoon, as light reflected off the Puget Sound, a customer ordered a cappuccino and a blueberry muffin from me. He was my age, with messy blond hair, a colorful sleeve of tattoos, and an expensive-looking messenger bag slung over one shoulder, filled with graphic design books. As I steamed his milk he asked, "So you're probably in fashion design, huh?"

"Excuse me?" I said over the hissing milk.

"What program are you in?" He laughed and picked at the top of his muffin. The milk screeched and I pulled it away from the wand.

"Oh, I'm in the espresso arts program," I said with a smirk. Pouring the foam into his cup, I saw the confusion on his face. "I mean, I just work here." I gestured at the small coffee stand around me.

"Oh, weird, I thought you had to be a student to work here." There was emphasis on the word *student*. Like he meant it to sting. "Most of the girls that work here *go* here." He adjusted the bag on his shoulder, collected his muffin and cappuccino, dropped some coins into my tip jar, and disappeared up the stairs that led to the classrooms.

The bus ride home felt bleak. If the sun was out downtown, it wasn't evident in north Seattle. When I saw the Futon Factory next to the liquor store, the landmarks that meant I was home, I pulled the cord. Inside the apartment I was restless. I opened the fridge two times, then a third, each time revealing the same tortillas and jam inside. This was the kind of afternoon that usually resulted in a trek across the busy highway to the pay phone.

I tugged at the strings of my hooded sweatshirt. Seattle was cold in June. Across the street from my apartment was a shopping complex. A Larry's Market, a Qdoba, a Starbucks, a Verizon Wireless, and a movie theater all huddled up against each other. I crossed the street in black sweatpants, rain boots, and a sweatshirt. I reached the curb, when a man in a station wagon waved me down. I was used to giving directions on the reservation. People usually got lost on their way to Anacortes. "Isn't there a ferry near here?" they'd ask from fancy Subarus or Land Rovers. "We're trying to get to the San Juan Islands."

I trotted up to the car and crouched down to the window. "Yeah?" I said, shivering a little in the wind.

"How much?" he said.

I rubbed my arms and shook a little. "Huh?" I looked around like I might find someone selling something.

"How much?" His hand was on his crotch and his lips mouthed the words *hand job*. He said it again, this time pawing aggressively at the bulge in his pants. "How much?"

I'd like to say I kicked the door of his car in. I'd like to say I shouted at him and made a scene, which later I would learn to do. Later, I became accustomed to the regularity of prostitution along Highway 99, but standing on the curb in front of the stranger's window, all I could do was back slowly away. All I could do was wonder in confusion why I was thinking about Julia Roberts in *Pretty Woman*, or why I was thinking about any prostitute in any movie I had ever seen. I stared down at my pajamas, perplexed. I wasn't in a rubber skirt, thigh-high stockings, or heels. I was a girl on the corner in her pajamas, a little confused and ultimately alone.

"I'm sending you some smoked salmon," my mom told me over the phone, days after the incident with the stranger. She was multitasking. I could hear dishwater running, the clanking of silverware. I was

happy about the fish but asked about the possibility
of a cell phone. I hated walking each morning across
the rushing highway to the pay phone. I hated the old
Buicks and Ford Cavaliers, their rusted bumpers and
tinted windows, the faces of men inside, but I didn't
tell my mom that. Instead, I asked about the whale.
My mother continued to follow the story and reported
the latest update while drying and putting the dishes
away. She reported that people were concerned that
it might get stuck in shallow water at low tide but that
it had made its way back to the open water of Pa-
dilla Bay. She said that the experts say gray whales
generally migrate along the coast at this time of year
to feeding grounds in Alaska, occasionally making
detours into western Washington's inland waters.

A screaming ambulance made its way down
Highway 99. A car rolled slowly along the curb, and
with my free hand I pulled my hood up over my head
and squeezed my body as close to the little wall of the
pay phone as I could get it. "I'm sure that whale will
be fine, honey." My mom was trying to reassure me.
"Don't worry about it too much."

That night, back in my apartment I pulled the duct
tape off the last box. It sat in the center of the linoleum with its big black letters: KITCHEN: POTS/
PANS. The cheap wooden cabinets splintered at the
edges, and I had to be careful each time I pulled

them open to shove more plastic plates and Tupperware into their new homes. I had four gray cups, two coffee mugs, four plastic plates with matching bowls, and two sets of silverware. I had one pot, which I would use mostly for ramen and box pasta. I had a single frying pan, which I would probably never use. Putting it away made my heart ache for my mom's fry bread. I closed the last creaking cabinet and went to bed.

In my dream I was behind the wheel of the silver 1985 Ford truck, the one I had learned to drive before I moved to the city. Sun bathed the familiar valley farm roads in soft yellow light. The rubber of the tires recognized the asphalt. I smiled as I passed the old farmhouse on Cedar Road. The hills circled the valley in a green half-moon of old growth. The highway curved along the shore, and the deep waters of the bay glittered cold and teal. Mount Baker was white in the distance. Had home always been so beautiful? Mountains, tidelands, and trees—had I never seen them like this before? Around the next corner would be the sign marking the turnoff to Swinomish, to Mom, Dad, brothers, and sister. In the golden light of the afternoon my right hand slipped slowly from the steering wheel and rose involuntarily into the air in front of me. I held it there. This is a gesture of gratitude in our tribe. But the next turn took me crashing beneath the icy surface of the Skagit River. The cold water broke around me as I sped into dark waters. The truck was now the slippery gray back of the whale, wounded and weather beaten. I dug my fingers into its slick body. Branches and pebbles whipped my face. My lungs ached and pounded for air.

My dream washed me up on the shores of the river. I woke shivering on a stony beach. I knew I was still dreaming when I felt the small hand of a girl child wrapped around my wrist. Just a few steps away from where my head lay on the cold, wet sand, I saw my great-grandmother's feet, the hem of her black skirt and her wool shawl. I stood up immediately to meet her, tried to wring out soaked hair, and without knowing why, tended to the child, picked river weeds from her pink cheeks, and wiped the mud and sand away. I scooted the small girl toward my great-grandmother, "This is your great-great-grandmother," I said excitedly. "She's a storyteller." We both looked up to my great-grandmother's face, but the old woman could not speak. She just smiled back at us, palm outward.

I woke and devoured a tortilla filled with butter and jam. I pulled on my jacket and rushed across the street. I dropped two quarters into the metal box and waited for my mom's voice. I asked about the family, about Grandma's health. We talked about the overcast skies in summer, her new teaching position. I chewed on the string of my hooded sweatshirt and sipped coffee from a paper cup. It was good to hear my mom's voice again. I recited the things I was supposed to say. I told her the apartment was great.

It was only one bus ride to downtown. My mother asked, "Are you okay?"

"I'm fine. I walked across the street to the coffee shop in my pajamas. The drivers around here are real jerks," I laughed, "but it's fine. I'm fine." I swallowed more coffee and asked, "Hey, what happened to that whale?"

"Oh, honey," my mom's voice fell over me like rain. "It died. It washed up somewhere near Lyman, big as the trunk of a cedar tree."

That night I lay in bed with images of whales above me. I saw them twisting and bending in the driftwood shallows of the river. I closed my eyes to the pale meat rotting on a riverbank. I pushed my toes into the sheets of my bed and wished for sand. The whale had washed up somewhere between Concrete and Lyman, a hundred miles from the ocean, lost and hungry. I felt my chest tighten, felt like I was drowning, when I thought of its last breath.

When I finally slept, I dreamt of the whale. It was alone on a deserted riverbank. The officials never came to claim it, to clean it up and take it away. Its flesh was pale, bloated, as the crows picked at it, carrying pieces of it away to their nests. I worked hard in my dream, through the afternoon, until daylight was moonlight. A deep red clay was mixed in a small pool at my feet. It was the same red paint we used in our longhouse ceremonies. The red paint is for healing. The clay covered my hands and I painted with my fingers, covering the rot and the places where giant bones were exposed. I painted using the words of my ancestors' language. I painted home, covering the giant animal in our names for mountains, rivers, valleys, and trees.

So they don't forget.

So we remember.

So you're never alone again.

First Salmon Ceremony

✳

"What kind of Indian are you?" my uncle asked as he dropped a thirty-pound fish into my arms. It was Christmas Eve. I was seventeen. He had instructed my cousins and me to join him in the driveway, and we dutifully lined up alongside his car on the icy pavement. Our gifts, he told us, were in the trunk. One by one he presented each of us with a massive salmon, straight from the trunk of his car, frozen and unwrapped. We exchanged nervous glances, bit down on our lips to keep from smirking or erupting into laughter. We probably wanted Discmans or gift certificates to the skate shop. We wanted something from the mall. We were teenagers. But instead, we held in our outstretched arms king salmon. I stood there, snow lightly falling on my blue hair, breath puffing from my black lips in cold clouds, and said quietly, "Uncle, I'm a vegetarian." This statement is what prompted his question. He shook his head as he turned around, asking once more before lumbering back up the driveway and into the house, "What kind of Indian are you?"

My uncle was an artist, a carver, a painter. He danced in the longhouse. He had an art studio in

Pioneer Square. His voice boomed when he spoke, and he wasn't afraid to yell at the kids. He called my mom Jilly Bean, and though he was often so stoic he was almost unapproachable, there was a softness about him, a deep care for us. He was ridiculously handsome too; a white woman once told him he looked like "a real Hollywood Indian." From a young age I'd been driven by an insatiable need to impress my *cool* but terrifying uncle. I drew him pictures. I wanted to be an artist like him, I'd say, before presenting him with stacks of what I thought passed for art. Once I even traced every page from my *Beauty and the Beast* coloring book, a small lie to impress my artist uncle. As I stood there in the snow, holding the salmon, I felt shame swell up in me. I wondered, *What kind of Indian am I?*

Shortly after that Christmas I sat in my Seattle apartment still wondering. The salmon was in the freezer, next to the vegan chicken nuggets and the Tofutti Cuties. I called my cousin, an engineering student at the University of Washington. He took the bus across the city with his sister, his backpack carrying his own fish and a six-pack of winter ale. Together we baked and ate the salmon. We laughed about pulling fish from the trunk of a car on Christmas. We reminisced about running barefoot along the Nooksack River as kids, building forts, putting on elaborate circus performances for bored relatives. We talked about the city, his school, my job at the busy restaurant. We'd both made it so far from the river. The salmon was *good*, good like when we were kids, good like we were transported back to summer gatherings surrounded by family, good like in the backyard of our great-grandmother's house, good like it was done the traditional way over a fire on ironwood stakes and not in the shitty oven of my basement apartment, no uncles or fathers tending coals, nothing but the posters of Nick Cave and Joy Division watching over us. We finished eating and drinking, played the last record on my turntable, and my cousins helped me clean up before we said goodbye. The fish had been my favorite gift that year, but I told no one, not my vegan roommates, not the vegan drummer I was dating. I kept my dietary transgression secret. The next day I threw the bones away so no one would see, but the question remained. As I closed the lid to the trash can, I knew I had done something wrong. I had been raised better than that.

My Coast Salish ancestors believed in honoring their food. It's hard to believe I am descended from people who celebrated their food so beautifully when I'm devouring a bowl of ramen, bought in a package of four for a dollar, unceremoniously on the couch while watching bad eighties and nineties movies in the dark, but that's my ceremony. Coast Salish tribes are salmon people. It's one of our main resources. The first salmon of the season was meant to be honored. The fish was carried on an ornate plank dressed in cedar boughs and sword ferns and brought into the longhouse with songs and dances. There was always a big feast following the ceremony in a tribal gymnasium where everyone came together, laughing, sharing stories, but most of all eating. Paper plates piled high with potatoes and greens, soft dinner rolls bought in bulk, and a giant piece of fish. I'd run through the grass along the water, climb the bleachers, horse around with the other kids. We'd line up along the big buffet tables. We'd wait for the elders to get their plates, then we'd rush the table in a frenzy, salivating over the metal chafing dishes, the piles of pink fish inside.

I have always been a shitty eater. As a child I favored plain cheese over pepperoni. I never wanted toppings. I picked things off my plate to dumb down the food. If it was Taco Bell, I only ever wanted a bean-and-cheese burrito, no onions. My palate didn't change as I reached my teens, but I did become vegetarian. When I was eleven, I spent a week at my uncle's home on the Nooksack River visiting my cousins. The land was big and curved along the river. Stretching meadows and old-growth forest made up the property, and my cousins and I swam in the river, ran along the trails, and picked berries. We found salmonberries and thimbleberries. We filled our fists with wild huckleberries and snuck into the raspberry fields across the farm road, filling up big metal mixing bowls that we would beg my aunt to turn into a pie. I have berries tattooed on me. Right next to my tattoo of the cassette recorder Agent Cooper uses in *Twin Peaks* I have a stem of thimbleberries inked into my skin. I also have blackberries and huckleberries, and a half sleeve of sword ferns decorating my body. Along with the terrible punk tattoos of my early twenties I have adorned myself with the things that mark me home. I didn't plan them out. It's as if my body knew it needed a map, a way to remember where I came from.

When I was eleven, I went to visit my uncle for a week and met a woman named Dream. My aunt and uncle had let her build a yurt on their land. My aunt and uncle had hippie friends, and the tribal land was big enough to let families build little cabins, homes, and yurts. Dream was intoxicating. Looking back, I may have had a small crush on her, this radical white woman with a sweet name who lived in the weirdest house I had ever seen. Dream was cool, knew about music, and had a nose ring. When dinner came, Dream did not have salmon but salad. Only salad. I was inspired by this. She was a strict vegetarian, and that night out on the Nooksack I passed on the fish that I loved and became a vegetarian. Perhaps if I could pass on fish I could pass on the bad things too, like the trailer we lived in on the reservation, the times we had no power or running water, the times our only food was from a can. Perhaps if I could stop eating animals I could grow up to be a woman alone, in a yurt, with a nose ring and a cool name.

My new diet stuck, even when Dream did not—

she eventually packed up her yurt and went on to whatever new white hippie adventure lay ahead. Maybe she went to Burning Man. Maybe she went to Santa Fe. My staunch vegetarianism remained, much to my mom's dismay; she let out a sigh and an eye roll every time her now twelve-year-old daughter said she couldn't in fact eat chicken enchiladas with the rest of the family.

My diet grew more strict after I left home. At fourteen I met the first boy I loved and together we figured out how to eat vegetarian as teen runaways. We asked for spare change until we had enough for a bag of forty-nine-cent burritos from Taco Bell. I remember the first home-cooked meal I made him, a cheese-and-pickle sandwich in our friend's kitchen at midnight.

The first girl I loved had a more refined palate. Together we'd sit on the curb of the Skagit Valley Food Co-op eating a picnic of French bread and spinach dip, hummus, and figs laid out at our feet like we were Grecian goddesses. In Seattle I met punks and activists. I fell for anarchists who devoted entire afternoons to making huge pots of lentils to supply whatever Food Not Bombs event was in the neighborhood. At the shows I went to I learned about PETA and heard stories of radical activism while a band's music rang out in the parking lot. While punks emptied entire cases of beer into themselves, they told me about factory farming and the evil realities of the dairy industry. Eventually I became vegan. It was only a matter of time.

But whenever I returned home to attend a gathering, I couldn't escape the smell of baking salmon. I eyed it along the buffet line as the elders went before me, huge servings of fresh pink salmon steaming on their paper plates. Everything about the fish made my mouth water, the silver skin and its scales, the white bubbles of fat oozing from its tender flesh. I would quiet my hunger with the tales of overfished oceans, of orca whales dying. I was doing the right thing, I told myself. But still the question clung to me each time I would politely mouth a *no thank you* to whoever was about to serve up a portion of salmon onto my plate. During the feast I'd look down at my sad meal—the iceberg lettuce, the mashed potatoes, and the Costco roll—my plate full but still so empty. I'd close my eyes to my uncle's disapproving face.

I ate hummus. I ate it all the time because I was always hungry. I didn't know what else to eat. I would come home from an eight-hour shift waiting tables, stand over my sink, and shovel handfuls of baby carrots and broccoli into my face. All the while, this huge fish-shaped hole began to grow in me, and no matter how many kale salads I ate I was starving. This is how I passively fell into a colonized diet.

My ancestors' diet was also colonized. Pre-contact they existed mainly on salmon, shellfish, wild berries, and bracken root. They ate things like elk. On reservations they were given commodity foods, things they had never had before, like lard, flour, salt, and canned beef. Once someone asked me what our traditional food was. "Indian tacos, right?" They were amused by this. "Fry bread? Right?" Wrong. This food was introduced to the first people post-contact. It's a colonized food. The people who lost their lands, their hunting and gathering places, the places they fished, were introduced to these foods by the U.S. government. Fry bread was what they came up with. It's a defeated food.

The first time I recognized commodity foods on television I was watching *Roseanne* with my white roommates. It was late. A band was sleeping over and we all huddled on the couch in my communal house in Seattle, sharing vegan pizza and beer. On TV, Roseanne opened the cupboard and yanked out a white bag with big black lettering that read POTATO CHIPS, bold and simple. "Oh my god," I laughed and pointed. "Look, reservation Lay's!" My mouth fell open in a dumb smile. I looked around at my friends, waiting for their joined laughter, that sound of a roomful of people all getting the joke. But the group was silent. Eventually a friend chimed in to say something about television series not having the rights to name brands. Something about licensing and endorsements. Something about Pepsi. The conversation shifted, but I couldn't stop thinking about the black-and-white cans of food, the black-and-white boxes and bags. I had seen the same label, the same black lettering against a white backdrop, when I was growing up on the reservation. FRUIT COCKTAIL in black and white. ORANGE JUICE, SHREDDED CHICKEN, APPLESAUCE, and even just MEAT in a can in a cupboard with dozens of other identical cans in my friend's house in the third grade. We had opened all the cans of peaches that day and eaten them in her driveway. That night I took some cultural inventory. None of my friends, my weirdo, disenfranchised, misfit, *white punk* friends, had ever seen a cupboard like that. I think of this every time one of my vegan friends examines a label, holds it close to their nose to read the long list of ingredients to determine whether the food in question meets their standards. This is a privilege. This is a luxury. I learned how to stay quiet. I learned how to stay hungry. I went to vegan grocery stores looking for what I craved. They had plant-based chicken, beef, and duck. They had every cheese imaginable made with cashews. But they never had salmon. The closest thing I ever found was a thin, unnaturally bright pink sheet of vegan lox. It was like a salmon-flavored fruit roll-up. It was awful. Still I spread it out on a bagel with vegan cream cheese, underwhelmed. I felt lonely as I ate it. I looked at its odd pink color and wondered how they made it. It's easy to accept that your diet has been colonized when you think you've chosen it.

In my teens and twenties, I convinced myself that if I somehow denied the part that made me Coast Salish, the part that made me Indian, I could be as carefree, radical, and punk as the people around me. That I could be more *white*. I didn't know how thoroughly being hungry would quiet me. I was quiet at dinner parties and on dates, at vegan potlucks and brunch outings. It always came back to "See, you don't have to eat animals. Look at what they're doing with soy and tempeh."

I hadn't realized how lonely I had been in my diet until my second year at the Institute of American Indian Arts, when I accidentally ate venison. I had joined the Students for Sustainability Leadership Program. I had a crush on the teacher, who maybe slightly reminded me of Dream, but she was cooler, like cared-about-wolves-and-listened-to-Neko-Case cooler. We planted traditional medicine gardens, raised campus awareness on climate change, and held recycled-fashion shows. Once a month we'd have a potluck, and at one of those I accidentally ate venison. When a vegan accidentally eats meat, it's usually followed by a stage-four meltdown, a fit of rage, and most likely a bad case of the shits. None of this happened to me. I was cruising along the buffet line, chatting with my teacher crush, and absentmindedly scooping things onto my plate. Grilled veggies, beans and rice, a tortilla, and finally a cup of red chili stew. We all sat at the big table in the student lounge excited about our upcoming projects. I took a giant spoonful of the red chili into my mouth, then another, and another. It was *good*. Halfway through my meal I began to wonder why my fellow sustainability leader was talking in detail about killing and dressing a deer. He kept motioning to the stew. With my mouth full of the delicious red chili, it occurred to me he had brought the stew. I sat with it on my tongue before swallowing. I looked at my friend as he continued his story of how he learned to hunt, how he was part of his tribe's hunting society, how he knew to use every part of the deer, even the hide.

With the stew still in my mouth I closed my eyes to the only memory I had of seeing a deer carcass. I hadn't yet moved to Seattle, but I was already dreaming of it. Instead, I had only made it twenty miles from the rez and into the woods, to a kind of punk rock Neverland. The white guys who built the cabin had also built a skate ramp, a huge half-pipe in the middle of the towering old growth. They held bonfires, punk bands played, and people partied. They prided themselves on living off-grid, on sticking it to the man. They had their own water system rigged up and a generator for power and were even working on a wood-burning soaking tub in the middle of the forest. One morning after a party I walked the trail that led to the creek. I stopped in my tracks. In the hot midmorning sun, a deer carcass was swinging from a rope above me. The smell rushed my face like a punch and I quickly covered my mouth, a fistful of vomit caught in my hand. I trembled before stepping back, unable to look away. Its dead eyes were dull and black, like two dark plums, dry and rotting. It hung from a tree in a cloud of flies, eviscerated, its flesh and guts pouring out onto the ground. A wave of nausea hit and I threw up again, this time onto my shoes. I ran to the creek still shaking. I fell to my knees and plunged my hands into the cold water, sobbing. The people who killed the deer were staying at the cabin, sleeping off a hangover. They had come to sell drugs and party and apparently to shoot things. I looked around my surroundings, at the old Icehouse cans, cigarette butts, and motorcycle parts littering the forest. What the hell was I doing out there? My *cool* friends, hell-bent on living off the land, making their own place in the woods, off-grid, had trashed the place, had killed something just to kill it.

I blinked the rotted deer from my mind and came back to the table, to my friend talking about his tribe's hunting society. He talked about how to properly dress a deer, how he had taken his time, how he had thanked the deer for its life. Then he talked about the stew itself, how he had roasted the chilis as his grandparents had shown him. I swallowed the stew. I wasn't grossed out or suffering from a stomachache or any guilt about having eaten the deer. Instead, I felt nourished in a way I hadn't in a long time. Like I was back at one of our tribe's feasts. I knew at that moment that I wanted to decolonize my diet.

My time at tribal art college in New Mexico opened up my diet to a world of traditional foods. I only ate meat if it was prepared indigenously. At the grocery store I still bought vegan, but through my school community there was an abundance of indigenous food. I tried elk and bison, and whale cut traditionally with an ulu. I drank Douglas fir–tip tea and found a book about traditional Coast Salish foods. I learned how to harvest nettles for stew and felt closer to food than I ever had.

But when I graduated and moved back to Seattle I was no longer surrounded by my indigenous peers. I tried to maintain my diet. It was useless. I found myself at a dinner party with friends. We all enjoyed a vegan stir-fry and I told the story about the venison. "Ew," the girl next to me interrupted, "that's horrible! You didn't spit it out?" A shame so big and heavy swelled up in me that I went quiet. I didn't know what to say; the faces of my friends, my non-indigenous friends, stared back at me. There was no indigenous meat around me. One morning, I found myself staring at a package of bison meat at Whole Foods. I held it in my hand, twenty dollars' worth of grass-fed, organic buffalo. I hated it. I hated the wild-caught salmon, the overpriced vegan options. I hated the looks on my white friends' faces whenever I talked about fish. While in the city, I had no idea how to decolonize my diet. I went back to my vegan ways.

When people ask me if I'm vegan, I'm still unsure

how to answer. I still don't support factory farming, or the dairy industry, and even if it were safe for me to eat, I have no desire to eat a once-living thing. Except salmon. I am wired to want this food. Like the genetically inherited high cholesterol passed down to me through my ancestors, I have inherited an appetite for salmon. I cannot shake this craving.

Last January I took the Californian I have been falling in love with to the beaches and rivers of the Pacific Northwest. I wanted to show him the water up here. He grew up tropical. He grew up in the sun. I wanted to share with him the gray stony shores of my childhood, the midnight-dark waves crashing on the jagged rocks. We drove to the Nooksack River first and camped along the water in the meadow. He met my favorite cousins; I picked him salmonberries and thimbleberries and he shivered when we jumped into the icy waters of the Nooksack. "This isn't California," I teased. My cousin showed me an ironwood stake he had carved, and we talked about the summer gatherings in our great-grandparents' yard.

Then I took him to the ocean, to a beach I have always loved. On our way we stopped at a trail in the Hoh Rain Forest. Near the northernmost point of Washington State, I stood with the Californian in the woods. He stepped over the wet roots and stones. He admired the old growth, the way everything here was draped in moss. I stood at a small wooden sign at the base of a berry bush. The sign identified the plant both in English and in the Quileute language. It read SALMONBERRY. I smiled at the word. As my date snapped photos of giant cedars and dew-covered sword ferns, I crouched down. I bent at the sign as if in prayer. My stomach rumbled for something that was not packed in our cooler full of fancy vegan snacks and kombucha beers.

We left the trail and headed to the beach. As the coast came into view we listened to moody synth music and snacked on hummus and crackers, but I couldn't stop thinking about salmon.

We neared a small reservation. I began to notice handwritten signs for smoked fish. I snapped like a rubber band. I pulled over and turned down "Catacombs" by Cold Cave on the stereo. My date eyed me suspiciously, curiously looking around, and asked me, "What's up?" I took in a breath. The Californian was a devout vegan. He had been for over a decade. I worried about what he might say. I worried about judgment. An embarrassing memory flooded my thoughts, still stinging, though it had been years. I'd brought smoked salmon to my ex-husband's family for dinner once. I was raised never to arrive empty-handed to a home where someone has invited you for a meal. I had brought my great-grandmother's smoked salmon dip. Proudly I set the dish on the counter and laid out the crackers. An exaggerated gasp came from the room over. "Ewww," my ex's mother complained, covering her nose and wafting the air dramatically with her hand. "Something stinks, did someone just open fish? It stinks!" There was emphasis on the word *stinks*. Quickly and shamefully, I tucked the offensive dip into the fridge, next to all the bougie Whole Foods groceries typically found in well-to-do white people's fridges. The fish spoiled in the fridge over the weekend. Before my ex and I packed up on Monday I washed the bowl out in the sink when no one was around to smell it. The hot water and lavender-scented suds erased the fish from my fingers.

Now, with my new date on the side of the road next to the gray ocean, I felt tears forming in the corners of my eyes before I launched into my statement. "I miss my family," I blurted out. "I miss my great-grandmother and my uncle. I miss my cousins and my great-grandparents' backyard." Cold Cave still droned in the background as my date looked back at me, concerned and curious. "I miss the way my uncle baked the salmon on the fire before my great-grandmother told stories." Tears were now streaming down my face. "I know you planned to make vegan clam chowder, and you know what, I *am* excited about that. But I want to eat a fucking salmon!" I said it defensively, poised for battle, my face red like children's after they cry.

The Californian laughed. It was a warm laugh, a sweet laugh. He shook his golden hair to one side and smiled at me. "Let's get you a frickin' salmon, babe." And just like that he eased the guilt, the shame, whatever had been growing in me since I was a teenager. My whole body had been stiff, rigid with defense. I felt it relax.

"Oh." I was stunned. "You're not grossed out? Or, like, mad or whatever? I'm totally breaking veganism." The Californian explained that he not only understood but supported it. He knew this was important to me. I was shocked, so used to the disapproving looks and combative judgment from my hard-core vegan friends. The Californian had surprised me. We drove into the small reservation, which looked like the reservation I grew up on: houses too close together, appliances decorating the lawns along with stacks of firewood. We followed the signs that read SMOKED FISH, until the arrows brought us up a driveway. An old fishing boat and rotted nets lined the garage. I smiled a big smile.

"This is where you get fish," I told him before enthusiastically hopping out of the car. I glanced back at my date, checking for any signs of hesitation or uneasiness. Up until that point I wasn't sure if he had ever even been on a reservation like this before. The one I lived on was tucked into the city of Tacoma, masked in urban sprawl. This was different. This was coastal. Fewer cafés and gas stations. Fewer white people. I looked back to find him totally at ease, working on freeing a tangle from his long hair as he stepped over discarded pieces of fishing equipment. My heart relaxed. An old man answered the door wearing a dirty white shirt and a big grin. We greeted each other and told each other where we were from. He nodded when I told him I was Upper Skagit and Nooksack. I told him I was looking for fish.

"My son's the only one fishing the river here now." He brought out his big plastic bins of fish. "No one else is doing it like him these days, not since I had the last stroke. Four strokes I've had. I'm not fishing anymore," he said matter-of-factly while laying out the different sizes of shrink-wrapped smoked salmon, a sense of pride on his face. I bought two big pieces and thanked him.

That night the Californian made his vegan clam chowder. I spread out salmon ceremoniously on a big dinner plate. I brought the fish out to the towering piles of driftwood and together we watched the waves as they crashed along the shore. I told him as best I could one of my great-grandmother's stories from memory. We drank fancy cocktails and played Scattergories next to a fire. I beat him. Twice. I had two servings of fish and he never mentioned the smell. This fish was good, soft and salty, covered in a thick glaze from being smoked. It broke apart in my mouth, melting. I closed my eyes to a rush of smoke. I was back at the salmon ceremony, I could smell the smoke rising up through the burning cedar, making its way through the body of the fish.

—

There is no more salmon east of the mountains in Washington State. Some Salish tribes are no longer able to practice their salmon ceremonies because the rivers are too polluted. They have to buy their salmon from someplace else. I thought about my salmon privilege, how foolish I had been to deny it. I walked to the water's edge and stood with my toes in the tide, my belly *finally* full of fish. As the waves ebbed at my ankles, the Californian joined me beneath the stars. He put his hand on the small of my back and told me he loved me. This time I heard it differently, heard it in a way that made me feel seen as a Coast Salish woman, as a woman who comes from salmon people.

When we celebrate the first salmon of the season, we honor it. We have dances and songs and a big feast. After the fish has been eaten, the people walk what's left of king salmon, his bones, his head, and his tail, back to the water and return him. They do this so his spirit can travel back to his people, to tell them how we honored him, to ensure his return. I began to wonder if my family would always be able to practice their salmon ceremony. I knelt down, with a fistful of the tiny white bones picked off my plate. Crouched down on the beach I emptied the small bones into the waves. I whispered into the darkness, thanking the fish, the man who caught it, and the ocean for its abundance.

This was *my* first salmon ceremony. It wasn't perfect. There were no songs or stories. My regalia wasn't woven from cedar. I stood in rolled-up jeans and a Joy Division T-shirt. Soon I would turn back and join the person I loved in our cabin, where we would play Judas Priest and dance before getting into a giant Jacuzzi. I felt a gratitude start to rise up in me, mixed with the faint grief I carried still. I mourned the time I had spent looking elsewhere for nourishment, and I grieved for the eleven-year-old kid who longed to be white, *all the way white*, the kind of white that lived in a yurt and knew about animal rights. I grieved for the girl who fell in love with anarchists and tethered herself to their values, for the silence she let herself learn. I grieved for not going to the Nooksack River enough, for not speaking my traditional language enough, for ever missing a single word my great-grandmother might have said. Mostly I grieved for ever not eating the salmon.

I thought about my uncle's question on Christmas. *What kind of Indian are you?*

I guess I'm the kind of Indian who will never be vegan, who will never again teach herself to be hungry or quiet. The kind who will bring the smelly salmon dip into your white fridge. I am the kind of Indian who will always be bad at making fry bread, who loves picking berries and driving along the coast listening to darkwave and synth-pop. I am the kind of Indian who will never hide who she is again and who will always eat the salmon.

As long as the salmon returns to us.

Cactus Flowers

❋

've never been a gardener. Growing up on a reservation in the Pacific Northwest, I never had to be. My backyard was lush with old growth. Towering cedars, moss-covered nurse logs, and sword ferns took up the space where flower beds might have been. My Coast Salish ancestors were not gardeners. They fished the rivers, picked wild huckleberries, and harvested cedar. To beautify a space by planting flowers wasn't something we practiced. To say growing up on the reservation was a privilege feels wrong, but the landscape of my childhood *was* remarkable. It may have been the reservation, a community founded on oppression, built by settler colonial trauma, but it was also a rainforest. It was coastal, rich with waterways, stony cliff sides, and windswept madrones. My backyard, as complicated as it may have been, was a paradise.

To uproot something is inherently traumatic. It says so on every potted hibiscus flower and jasmine start I've put in the ground. The instructions are simple: Handle the root system with care, and be gentle while arranging it into its new home. Transplanting shocks the plant, but with enough care it will adapt.

I've been adapting to my partner's home in Southern California. I've been handling myself with care. But my roots are up the coast, solidly grounded in the wet earth. I have left my ancestral homeland, and the transition has been rocky.

When I arrived, I was still dreaming of home, my dreams of beaches so vivid I could feel the slate-gray sand beneath my feet and the cold mist on my face. I blinked my partner's bedroom, *our bedroom*, into focus, shocked to find myself in our bright space. *Oh yeah*, I realized. *Here I am.*

To combat homesickness, I decorated. I brought my grandmother's cedar baskets and my uncle's paintings of longhouse ceremonies. I hung a decal of a forest, and ferns and plants that climbed their vines along my ceiling. We call this my Northwest Room. It's part *Twin Peaks*, part Coast Salish cultural exhibit, and part shrine to the bands of my teenager-hood. I created an imitation home, one that proved useless when I woke up missing the sound of rain, the smell of wet dirt.

I used to walk for miles behind my house in old growth, on trails along streams and salmonberries. San Diego is different. We enter our yard through the neighbor's driveway. Beyond our gate are hot pavement, palm trees, and corner stores. There is an element of convenience here, a bike ride away from a great bookstore and amazing burritos. But even frolicking in the turquoise water of La Jolla, warm as bathwater, I missed the harsher beaches of my child-hood, full of stones and driftwood. I missed the bite of the Salish Sea in mid-July.

One afternoon I broke down in tears, over-whelmed by my displacement. Sometimes as a Native person it's too heavy to feel far away from ancestral places. When my partner asked me what I might need to feel more at home here, I surprised myself by saying, through tears and laughter, "I need to Weedwack the yard." I realized I hated the yard. The itchy crabgrass looked nothing like home so I erased the yard from existence. It was just a place I had to traverse in order to reach the front door. The weeds were overgrown and reached my hips, so saturated in dog urine that the entire yard was permeated in pee.

We bought a Weedwacker, and I spent a week digging in the yard. I unearthed piles of fossilized dog shit and trash. I discovered two rose bushes, a brick-lined flower bed, and terra-cotta pots with cac-tus plants still growing in them. Beneath the weeds I found a succulent garden struggling for sunlight. I marveled at the most sci-fi garden box I'd ever seen. Hot pink and neon green foliage reached upward like tentacles. Spiky tendrils, more weapon than plant, climbed up out of concrete. They had been here all this time and had somehow survived.

At first the garden was just a distraction, a way to keep busy while I wasn't teaching or writing. Each morning I checked on my sci-fi garden, delighted to see the strange plants thriving. I learned that the fire-stick plant is toxic to dogs and removed it, planting safer succulents in its place. On walks with my dog, I filled tote bags with clippings. I found a prickly pear cactus growing in a ditch and collected pieces to add to my garden. Was I stealing plants? I'm not really sure. I mostly just took small pieces growing in public spaces and never enough to notice. I was fascinated by them, how you could pluck them from their homes, and with a little water and sunlight they'd come back strong. I fell in love with their resilience, their ability to adapt, to withstand drought and displacement. It's amazing how little these plants needed in order to become strong again.

I filled the yard with jade pinwheels, ghost plants, and burro's tails. I planted hibiscus and night-blooming jasmine. The yard no longer smelled like urine but fragrant and floral. We repurposed things left by previous tenants. An old door became a plant shelf. I trained bougainvillea to grow around a rusted fire gate. The yard began to feel like a sanctuary.

My mother gave me a book when I was nine or ten. *Mandy* is the story of an orphan who runs away and stumbles upon an abandoned cottage in the middle of a forest. She fixes it up, learns to garden, and makes it her own. I loved this book as a kid, intoxicated by the fantasy of making a *home* out of nothing, out of abandonment. In her yellow dress, Mandy kneels in the dirt and the flowers; the tagline floating below reads, *The magic of finding a home.*

"You can always go back," my partner said to me one sunny afternoon in the park by our San Diego house. He closed the book he had been reading, and when he spoke to me there were tears in his eyes. "To your ancestral home," he went on. "Keep your house in Tacoma. We can live in both places." I realized the book he had been reading was one of my favorite novels, one about connection to land and ancestry, and I knew what he meant. I trusted that he would never keep me from returning to the Pacific Northwest if the missing got too bad, or if I simply needed to revisit the rain and the old growth. I think you fall in love with the same person dozens of times throughout the course of a relationship, and that afternoon in the sunlit grass I felt the pull in my heart toward him again.

I watched June's strawberry moon rise from my garden. I remembered my great-grandmother. Her family followed the supply of salmon and berries. They moved up and down the Skagit River. Her mother brought a piece of linoleum and laid it down on the dirt or sand to create a home wherever they were. I looked at my salvaged door turned shelf, the cactus flowers in desert pinks and pale greens, the blooms out of place and strangely beautiful encased in spikes. A group of blue-crowned parrots flew overhead, chirping as they passed. My partner gently

removed spines of a bunny ears cactus from my fingertips. We laughed at how bad I was at collecting
cacti. We promised to get better gloves. I looked at
this space we had created and I realized I was closer
to home than I'd ever been.

Si?aƛ': Orations: 4

✳

These shores will swarm with the invisible dead of my tribe, and when your children's children think themselves alone in the field, the store, the shop, upon the highway, or in the silence of the pathless woods, they will not be alone. In all the earth there is no place dedicated to solitude. At night when the streets of your cities and villages are silent and you think them deserted, they will throng with the returning hosts that once filled them and still love this beautiful land. The White Man will never be alone.*

Chief Seattle witnessed the arrival of Captain George Vancouver, one of the first British explorers to arrive in Coast Salish territory. It was the chief's intuitive response to welcome the white ships, ships that later brought diseases his people had never encountered. Influenza, measles, and

smallpox nearly decimated the indigenous popula-
tion of the Pacific Northwest.

—

When the pandemic hit, I was unreasonably fearful.
My partner tried to console me as I shivered in the
spring daylight that poured in through the windows
of my kitchen. I held a peony in one hand and a
drugstore thermometer in the other. The word *epidemic* carved itself into my brain and stayed there. I
thought of ghosts. I thought of smallpox. I cried to
my partner. *I'm not sick. I'm afraid.* It was a hardwired
memory. As the news reported record numbers of
people dying, I marched back and forth, wracked
with worry. *No, I won't sit still. No, I don't have a fever.
Don't you get it. Aren't you listening?* My survival instinct
was drumming inside.

We've been here.
We've been here.
We've been here before.

Licorice Fern

My mother and I recently attended a Native art market outside Tacoma. As we wove in and out of the booths in the hot sun, I watched as she greeted the vendors, some of them friends or folks who have participated in the language conference my mom puts on every year in Seattle, others strangers. They smiled and spoke traditional greetings to one another. I stood back as my mom admired a pair of cedar woven earrings that matched the pendant she wore that day. She held them up to her face and smiled at me. I gave a nod of approval and told her if she didn't get them, I would. We both laughed as the friend who made them joined in and bagged them up for her. The day was hot and breezy. I watched as young children ran around the tables and played as their parents sold their traditional beadwork, weavings, and paintings. My mom seemed at ease, joking and making polite conversation in Lushootseed. It was good to see her like that, happy and in her element. On the short car ride home, we talked about my writing and her work at the Seattle Indian Health Board. We exchanged stories heavy with emotion, how the essays I was tackling were weighing on me, how her own strained relationship with her mother was taking an emotional toll. We spoke to each other openly and honestly. It hasn't always been that way.

A professor once asked me after reading an early draft of my memoir, *But where were your parents?* I was stunned by the inquiry. Surely I had included them. They had been part of my story. But my professor highlighted the end of one section, then the beginning of the next. *You go from age ten, safe with your family, then suddenly, you're alone at fourteen. You're sleeping in parking lots and bowling alleys.* Where *were your* parents? The question ignited a powder keg of unwanted memories, of all the things I'd been avoiding.

They were around, I shrugged. *They were busy.* I drove home from our meeting pummeled by the weight of her question. *Where?* I went over the timeline. The narrative, *my* narrative. At ten I was assaulted. Shortly after that, we moved from the trailer into a church attic. Then a new home. Then I began running away. At first just one town over. Then eventually to Seattle. I acted out. I shaved my head and stopped coming home. The memories busted me open. That afternoon I cried as I drove away from campus, gripping my steering wheel. I went back to the memory of it, to the memory of the first break.

My mom's red car is sailing through the valley farm roads.

I'm fourteen. My mom, who's more big sister than mom, is beautiful, drop-dead gorgeous really. She's talking openly as a sea of pink tulips floats outside her window. The rows of tulips happen every year, transforming the valley into an ocean of color.

We're driving from Swinomish to Mount Vernon. We're on our way to my first day at the alternative high school I've chosen to transfer to. We have had a fight, not unusual for the time, and we are "processing." When you're raised by a tribal social worker, a woman who deals with trauma on a daily basis, a woman who spends most of her time as a counselor, you learn to do a lot of processing.

I'm still "lashing out," I think is how she puts it. The pale pink tulips begin to darken. The rows of flowers stretch out for miles, and this is where she breaks down. This is where she cries and tells me she's relapsed. I focus now on the magenta sprawl of petals behind her head. Relapsed? The flowers change to a deep fuchsia. She tells me about the abuse that happened to her as a child, the ways she learned to self-medicate. I already know about the abuse. A man. A grandfather. A body and face I had never seen had hurt her when she was small. She had divulged this information after my own body had been violated, in an effort to console me. But this new information is about pills and drinking in secret. This is the first time my mother tells me openly about alcohol and medication. The way she'd use them in total secrecy. Hidden from her colleagues, her husband, her family.

My mother talks about the ways she kept it hidden, staying some nights at a friend's apartment in the city. She'd call home to tell her family she had a late night at work and couldn't make the hour commute home. I think of bad husbands in movies calling their wives to tell them they were going to "stay late at the office tonight" so they could sleep with their young secretaries. Were the pills and alcohol so much more attractive than us? Her family? The petals fade to a deep violet.

I never saw my mother drunk. Never saw her high on pills. Opiates. Painkillers. This is because she is also addicted to secrets, the silence of them. I never saw her falling down or stumbling. I only ever saw the woman who graduated from the University of Washington, who went into tribal social work, who was loved by my great-grandmother. I only saw the woman who made me a bowl of German chocolate ice cream and curled up on the couch with me to watch Gigi *when I was sick, who took me out for a strawberry milkshake when I got my period, who made me a mermaid-shaped cake, painted a denim jacket for me, and told me I was a beautiful girl.*

Now a wall of tulips fades behind her. The violet shade of their petals is so dark that they're practically black; this is the only tulip I've ever admitted to liking. As teenagers, my friends and I loathed the tulips. "They really are an ugly flower," I'd say. We hated the busloads of people with cameras the tulips brought to our small town. We hated the street fair and its awful handcrafted garbage. We hated watercolors of daffodils. They also planted daffodils in the valley. Though the tulips were the main attraction, some fields were butter-yellow lakes of daffodils. We hated calendars of Skagit Valley, carved wood tulips, and even the singular smokestack in Mount Vernon's small downtown, painted as one big, concrete tulip.

These black flowers behind my mother's face remain to this day the only tulip I'll tolerate. And as she tells me these things, the stupid flowers are all I can think about. It's the first time I've ever really wanted to cry and don't. I'm quiet as I look at them. Soon the tourists will come and go. Soon the petals will drop to the dirt and the valley will go back to green and brown and then gray.

The last field is the sunshine color of daffodils, their bright yellow petals like stars, their insides an orange core, like something exploding. Opposite this field I see another. This one an alarming sea of vermilion and orange. Fire tulips. Their petals, the delicate flames of them, look like they are engulfing the valley in a raging explosion. Eating it. Swallowing it. Scorched farmhouses and smoke are all I see. I look instead at the gray pavement of the highway as it takes us miles away from the flowers. I think of the town ahead, the city beyond it, and feel orphaned.

After that car ride with the tulips, I saw my parents less and less. I worked hard to create something in their absence. I filled the parent-shaped hole in my life with a new family. At fifteen I had an apartment with six friends, punks, weirdos, and musicians. Occasionally I would hitchhike one town over, back to the reservation, and visit my parents. But something had changed. We were quiet in our small talk. We had crossed some threshold and there was no undoing what had been done. When we spoke, I withheld things. I never told my mother about the ways I had been hurt since leaving home. I spared her the details because I worried she had enough on her plate already. By seventeen I had already survived two assaults, an abusive relationship, and date rape. I kept these stories from my mother, not knowing that I was trying to protect her. I weathered the storm and carried the pain for both of us. I didn't realize at the time that I feared for my mother's safety, her sobriety. I chose silence because I worried we might once again find ourselves in that car with the tulips and the confession.

My mother had confessed to me that she had been hurt in the same way I had when I was young, that she had learned to self-medicate. The idea of my mother feeling alone, feeling the isolation and the shame that I had, haunted me more than my own memories of assault. I hated that she had learned to survive in a way that sometimes took her away from me. In my teenage years my compassion and my empathy were masked by rage. We'd have screaming matches and big blowouts. It was easier to leave than to face the complexity of my pain; the truth that I felt unprotected by her or that she had somehow failed me as a parent was too big to unpack at fourteen.

I have a memory of my mother when I was only six years old. We were living in the U District with my grandmother, as my mom worked hard to finish her degree, and she was committed to her sobriety.

As my brother and I roughhoused on the high deck hanging over the driveway, I lost my footing and fell. I crashed onto the pavement and shattered the bone in my arm. That day my mother had to skip classes to rush me to the hospital. After they set the break and put on the cast, my mother bought me a milkshake and a pink plastic My Little Pony. I can remember how she looked, every detail. Her long dark hair was teased big, her shimmery blue eye shadow sparkled in the sunlight. Despite the injury, it's one of my most cherished memories. It was a time when there was nothing between us; it was simply a mother-and-daughter memory.

When I was an adult, my mother came to visit me in Santa Fe, where I was finishing my undergraduate degree at the Institute of American Indian Arts. I remember being delighted that my mother had come to see me. The visit felt special. I was thrilled to show her my scholarship awards, the portrait of me hanging on the wall of academic achievement. We had come a long way from the fishnets and years spent running away. I felt compelled to prove something to her, to point at all the ways I had turned out okay despite everything. At the time, I was living in a big house close to campus and had six roommates. My mom and I shared my bed, and I remember feeling the way I did that day with the milkshake and the broken arm. My mom and I fell asleep watching a movie in bed and there was a closeness between us that felt delicate. Before the week was up we met her childhood friend for dinner on the plaza. I listened as they swapped stories, my mom smiling, face lit up in memory. Then like a freight train crashing into our fancy dinner table sending the cutlery and the glass-ware crashing into a thousand tiny pieces, my mother ordered a glass of champagne. Not two, not three, not a bottle—just one glass. But the glass was enough to send my inner fourteen-year-old self flailing. My stomach twisted and I sat frozen, unsure of what to say to my adult mother, in front of her adult friend, so I stayed silent. I went to bed feeling guilty, feeling torn up and confused. We didn't talk about the glass of champagne until months later, when my mom did something she had done numerous times and pulled out a letter and made her amends to me in the mall parking lot.

Over twenty years have passed since the tulip car ride, and I live for the first time since childhood in close proximity to my parents. Ours has been a slow and cautious rebuild. The first time my mother and I walked in Swan Creek together, I was reluctant to go. I had been bedridden for days, holed up in the half-empty bedroom of my new home in Tacoma. I had been unpacking for weeks, hell-bent on making the empty house a home. I didn't want help. That was part of it. For days I lifted heavy boxes, moved fur-niture from room to room, convinced the indepen-dence was what I needed. It was partly about control.

It was about my loneliness and my surroundings. I decided where every painting would go. I played Tetris with room layouts and bulky sofas. I organized all the books on the shelves by color, a literary rainbow in my office that I had always wanted. For the first time in my life, it felt like everything was up to me.

Then one afternoon as I bent forward to gather my cat into her carrier to go to the vet, I felt a pain so intense I saw stars. *Pinch* is not the right word. It was more like a tear, a ripping somewhere deep in my body. For a minute I lay frozen on the floor trying to determine the severity of my injury. Peesh Peesh paced back and forth, mewing in pain from a UTI. *Shit*, I huffed and dragged myself up using the back of a chair. Then, because sometimes I'm so stubborn it makes me stupid, I ate an eight-hundred-milligram ibuprofen and loaded her gently into the back of my car. I winced in pain the entire way. When I turned corners, I cried out. I took everything in deep breaths and intervals, counting to ten over and over and telling myself, *You can make it. You have to, because your stupid cat needs you.*

When I got home, I climbed carefully up the stairs. I stepped out of my clothes as I ran a bath. Then the small movement of bending forward to shut off the water sent pain shooting through my entire body. It was worse than picking up Peesh Peesh, and I crashed onto my bathroom floor bare-assed and crying. I dragged myself across the floor. When I tried to stand, something was wrong. Something was off in my body and no amount of ibuprofen was going to fix anything. When I made it to my bed, I gripped the high metal frame. I did a full pull-up, something I've never been able to do, and for a moment was distracted by how impressed with myself I was. I craned my neck to look at my backside. The muscle I could see was *jumping*. It was moving and twitching, vibrating just beneath my skin, and I had to bite down to keep from screaming. I called my only friend in the city. *Raine*, I said more embarrassed than afraid, *I can't even pull up my own pants.*

Raine was standing above me in under ten minutes taking inventory. They helped me into my clothes, and each bend and lean was excruciating. I decided I didn't want to go to the hospital. *I'll drive myself to the walk-in clinic in the morning, when it's affordable.* But as Raine helped me into bed, they frowned and said, *I'm calling your mom.*

NO WAY! I protested, but it's hard to oppose anything when you can't even sit upright for dramatic effect. Raine just shook their head and grabbed my phone. *Yep, sorry.*

That night my mother came over and looked after me. It was a strange kind of defeat, to be a grown woman, who left home at fourteen, who emancipated herself at fifteen, to succumb to the fact that her mother has to help her with every single bodily movement. My mother slept next to me, on my queen bed, surrounded by boxes and yet-to-be-hung paintings. It was hard not to think back to our Santa Fe sleepover, how close it had felt, how quickly it came undone. I held my breath for the break, the crash that I knew would follow. I braced myself for it. First thing in the morning, she drove me to urgent care, where they gave me a steroid shot in my back and told me I had torn something. It was spasming. My mom helped me back to the car and had to move my limbs into a sitting position for me.

After days in bed, I was able to move around. I took small walks around the house and cringed at the half-finished things. It hurt to try to hang things. I got stir-crazy. I felt like a prisoner in an undone home. When my mom sent a text to ask me if I wanted to walk in Swan Creek, I wasn't sure. I remembered the dinner in Santa Fe. I wondered what awaited me on those trails. I had been so aware of the thing wedged between our bodies the night my mother had to sleep next to me. Like a knife-shaped vulnerability, quiet and stinging. I had nightmares of my bones crumbling and filling up the bed, turning it into a beach of broken seashells. I knew this was partly to do with the pain, but it was partly about our history.

I was on edge and I couldn't put my finger on it. Of course I remembered things. Fights and the afternoon my mother sat me down on the porch with a pack of Pall Malls when I was thirteen. She had caught me smoking and thought this would cure me.

I was green by the time I smoked the last one, but all I gained was an affinity for chain-smoking. There were screaming matches and tears. The night she had to drag me from the back of our van across the pavement and into the emergency room after I downed a bottle of aspirin with alcohol. The psych ward and therapy. By age thirteen, a runaway. And finally, a court-approved emancipation at fifteen.

I wasn't used to my mother being readily available to take care of me. Wasn't used to offers to go for walks or to her asking if I needed food or a cup of coffee. So I paced around the house with my phone in hand. There were so many things I wanted to say. I typed them out and deleted them. I did this over and over, overcomplicating a simple answer as to why I could or could not walk in Swan Creek at that particular moment. I wasn't sure if I wanted to talk about it or how I would begin to explain why her care and nurturing the other night had made me so uncomfortable. I typed out direct phrases: *Sometimes I feel like you were never my mother and that's okay.* Then I deleted and tried again: *You've always been more like a big sister.* Then a stream of sentences: *It's hard to talk to you. Sometimes you don't say anything when I need you to. I wish we didn't have to talk about your sobriety as much as we do. I don't think you understand what I'm going through. Sometimes I think you're mad at me and I'm not sure why.* And finally: *Are you even proud of me?* Then I deleted everything and responded simply: *Yes, I'll go to Swan Creek.*

Our first walk in Swan Creek was quiet. We made small talk. *How is your back? Are you liking your job with the Puyallup tribe?* We talked about the little things, because the big things took up too much space. I didn't tell her the things I was struggling with because I didn't feel like there was enough space on the switchbacks for both of us.

Right before I emancipated myself, I went home to visit. I was already living in an apartment in a town twenty minutes away from the reservation. I was fourteen, and as my mother and I talked on the porch she said something to me. I don't remember the details of our conversation, but I remember the feeling of being fourteen and hearing the words from the adult as she said them. *You're so much smarter than me.* It was a black hole imploding and sucking every part of me into nothing. It was the obliteration of safety all over again. We were both crying when I left that night, and I'm still not sure if I know what it means. Because I was the kid. And she was the mother. I was carrying my wallet, a pack of cigarettes (not Pall Malls), and a Discman in a vintage lunch pail. I was dressed in fishnets and sneakers. But if I had to guess, I think, or I hope, that what she meant was that she loved me. Was that I was going to be okay, no matter what. But on that trail on our first walk in Swan Creek, I was remembering that night and I wanted to say to her, *Maybe I was smarter because you raised me.*

There have been times in my life where my mother

feels far away, unreachable. Once when I was still a teenager my family gathered on Easter Sunday. I remember being annoyed because I had to hitchhike and take a bus from my apartment. My brother was there with his kids, and my other siblings hung out as the little ones hunted for eggs in the yard. My mother had just come back from rehab. And I watched as she helped my nieces fill their pastel baskets. She moved slowly, but she was smiling. She looked relieved to be home. I sat on the porch and watched her for a while, wondering how hard it must have been to face her addiction, to go away for twenty-eight days, only to have to come home and decorate eggs. My mother deserves a medal for that day. And I try to remind myself that she somehow knew before I did that I'd be okay. She likes to say to me, *You're so smart, and you can do anything.*

But that day in Swan Creek a sort of softness happened between us. I was rigid with worry, expecting news or some new revelation that would once again remind me that I was alone. That the mother I had was gone, missing in her own healing. I braced myself for something I had learned to do at a young age, to worry and wonder about my mother, to tiptoe and be careful. I left home when most daughters still clung to their mothers for approval, for advice about love and bodies and makeup. In my leaving I never stopped to consider why my parents had failed me as parents. I was too busy learning how to find my own safety. I was building a home, a safety net, I was Peter

Pan and all of the Lost Boys at once. I didn't need grown-ups. But my emancipation and sudden adulthood also forced me into the role of Wendy. I had to take care of myself and sometimes the people around me. I was exhausted, too tired to reflect on what it must have been like to be two struggling Coast Salish parents, young, on the reservation, battling their own pasts and histories of substance abuse. And though she slipped up occasionally, my mother won her own safety; she fought against the capacity we as Coast Salish women have for disappearing, and she came out on top. I think of my parents, as complicated as our relationship might be at times, as heroes, as a place I look toward for strength.

A week after that first walk, my mom and I went again. Then again. The walks in Swan Creek became a ritual of ours, one that feels strange to miss if I'm out of town traveling or visiting my partner in California. Sometimes when I'm gone too long, we substitute our weekly trail walking with a phone call. And we *talk*. We share things, we're open. We don't hold back. As Native people, my parents have had to learn to fight. They carry the weight of generations on their backs, and as Native people often do, they've had to learn to heal, to carry wounds in a way that does not break them.

When non-Native friends comment on the relationship I have with my mother, I take it with a grain of Salish Sea salt. I don't let it in. Because white friends don't understand what it's like to come from generational trauma or the way an attempted erasure can live in our bodies and move through us. It is an active healing between us. And we work at it every day. When I think back to the first break, the moment I thought I had lost my mother, all I can remember are the tulips. I see the rows and rows of them spanning the valley in a rainbow of color. That valley was once our ancestors' tidelands, their waterways, their places of harvesting and abundance. The tulips happen every year, a petal flag of settler colonial triumph, a reminder that shouts, *You lost.* When I remember my mother's words, the confession of feeling broken, the tulips frame her profile. And I think to myself, *And why wouldn't you be? Look at the land, look at our families. Look at how we've had to carve out our own existence against a world that wished to erase us.*

I have compassion for my mother, and it does not translate as rage these days. I see her wounds reflected in my own. I understand the way they worked to keep us quiet. And when my mother invites me to salmon gatherings and Native art markets, I see the wounds being sutured. I see community and abundance, kinship and healing. And we still walk in Swan Creek every week that I am home in the Pacific Northwest. I see her in a different way: no longer shrouded in the colonial petals of primary-color tulips but blanketed in Native plant medicines. All around her on the switchbacks are sword ferns, stinging nettles, and salmonberries. Her face is beautiful as she speaks, surrounded by rich green. I erase the memory of the car and the tulips. I make a new one.

I watch my mother walk the switchbacks down to the creek. Some days she kneels forward and picks up broken things, pieces of glass and discarded cans, and she fills up her bag with the trash that litters this place. This isn't her job, but she does it anyway. Today she is gathering plant medicine. She stops, leans forward, and returns with a fistful of salal berries. These have so much protein, she tells me. Here, try one. And the berry is sweet and dark and tastes like candy.

We pass a cluster of flowers, bright pink, orange, and yellow. I close my eyes and remember my brother and me alone as toddlers, eating a rainbow of cereal off the ground like animals. I remember that Easter Sunday, with the kids and the painted eggs. I follow my mom close to the water, where she carefully harvests bushels of stinging nettles. These are good for soothing pain, she tells me, and are delicious for eating. We have to wear gloves when we gather them because the leaves sting and burn and leave welts on the skin. But if you use the plant on deep aches and arthritis, she says, it acts as an anti-inflammatory.

In Swan Creek we gather Douglas fir tips and pick salmonberries. We fill my mother's bag depending on the season. She knows how to make salve out of cottonwood. Rub this on scrapes and bruises, she tells me, because it's soothing. To ease the pain.

And as we climb back up the trail, I remember that day when I was fourteen. I go back to the moment in the car with the tulips, to the child me hearing my mother's confession. And I look at the woman gathering plant medicines, telling me new things. Not about addiction or secrets but about healing. Somewhere deep down there is a child me meeting her mother for the first time. And it's late, but it's not never, and when neither of us were paying attention, she became the parent. It happened here, on these trails.

My mother comes to a large tree and delicately pulls at the roots of a small fern. She tells me this is a licorice fern. Its healing properties are respiratory. And she shows me how to gently remove the plant from the moss. Then she tells me a story.

Our tribe knows this plant because once there was a woman in a village who was mute. She had no voice. One day as she walked in the woods, the little plant called to her. If you chew my roots, it said, I will give you back your voice. The woman did as the plant instructed and chewed the sweet-tasting root. Her voice returned to her and she brought the plant back to her people. She told them that if they ever felt they couldn't speak or communicate what they needed to, the plant would give their voices back to them.

I fill my mother's canvas bag with licorice fern, and she promises to teach me how to make tea. "It'll be good for your asthma," she says, smiling and patting her chest. I smile back and think of the silence that had taken root between us, and the separation it caused. I think of all the times I had wished so hard to tell her things. I know that the licorice fern will be good for both of us, for our strength to finally use our voices, even when the things we have to say are unspeakable.

River Silt

There is a photo of me when I was much younger. I am standing with my cousin next to the burning embers of a dying campfire. We are both barefoot, our toes covered in soot and sand, and I am holding a stick and smiling big. *You look like wild children*, a friend commented beneath the photo on social media. Then a smiley face followed by *This is so Lord of the Flies* and finally, *Lol, where are the adults?* It's true, the photo is lacking grown-ups. And my cousin is butt-naked and maybe five years old. I'm eight, wearing a black-and-yellow polka-dot bathing suit under a filthy Canadian tuxedo: dirty denim jeans and a dirty denim jacket.

We were always covered in dirt along the river. We dug holes into the muddy banks and used sticks and wet clay to construct our forts. We used shells as shovels and carved thrones into the cliff sides. Being dirty along the river are some of my happiest memories. We cooked salmon on ironwood stakes over the fire and listened to the stories my great-grandmother told, our hands sticky with sap as we ate marshmallows straight out of the bag. Sometimes we dragged our sleeping bags from our tents out into the meadow grass and fell asleep watching the stars. We always left the river filthy and smelling like smoke. We left exhausted and happy.

The first time I heard a girl say another girl was gross because she smelled like fish, because she smelled dirty, I thought it was a good thing. I was in the third grade, and to me fish smelled good. It reminded me of the river and nights around the campfire. "Don't talk to her," the girl instructed the others, "she's dirty." The offensive-smelling girl was kind, she lived down the street from me on the reservation, and I worried for the first time whether I also smelled bad. I huffed my hair. I sniffed my jacket. I found the scent of campfire smoke there. The girl who made the rules was pretty and white. She didn't live on the reservation, and I wondered how I was able to skirt the edges of her popular-girl circle. I realize now, as an adult, that it was because of the half of me that was white, the half of me that wasn't Indian or from the river. And it wasn't the lingering campfire in our hair or the smell of smoked fish on our fingers. She was talking about our bodies, about something deep inside of us that had gone bad.

At nine years old I didn't understand what could make girls be so mean to each other. They whispered stories about the girl who lived down the street from me. They refused to invite her to birthdays or slumber parties. There was an emphasis on the girl's body, the space between her legs. So I checked between my legs when I was alone. I sniffed my body's scent from my fingers and found it tart like fruit that wasn't ripe. I became scared of that part of me, afraid that it might become dirty and that everyone would know.

At seventeen I was far away from the river in a basement apartment in Seattle. I dragged my body to the shower and pulled myself up on the metal handle. The water was hot and I cranked the knob as far as it would go. I rested my weight on the tiled wall and watched blood swirl the drain, ribboning against the bright white steam. Back in bed I curled my body into a cannonball. I smelled lavender and eucalyptus. I could hear him in the living room. He was watching skate videos.

There is another version of this memory; it's the one I looped in my head like a nursery rhyme. It's all I could do to anesthetize the stinging pain between my legs, the ache of the bruises that had already begun to bloom across my thighs in the shapes of his fingertips. In this version, he never leapt off me. I never saw something like disgust flash across his face before quickly twisting into anger. He never gathered up all the covers and stormed out. He never shouted that I had overreacted, that I was fine, or that the blood that pooled beneath me repulsed him. In this version, my body's bedtime story, he stays. He apologizes for not listening when I said no and gently carries me to the shower. He says he's sorry a dozen times and he crawls into the steam with me. He washes my body, even the parts that burn and sting. Then he tucks me in clean, not dirty.

When I was twenty, I slept with a guy who always wanted to take baths with me. I thought it romantic at first, the candles and the clouds of bubbles. But I couldn't help but wonder if he made me bathe each night to ensure that I was clean. I worried he thought my body was too dirty to love and disguised the cleaning ritual as something beautiful. It haunted me every time. I had to wash before he touched me.

I often wondered if the white settler, a Scottish sea captain who married my Chinook ancestor, thought her dirty. After all, he kept her in the shed, a small structure with four walls, a dirt floor, and one window. She wasn't allowed in the main house. She was his wife and the mother of his children, but she was also an Indian woman. She came from the river, someone who knew how to harvest camas root, how to weave cedar rope and prepare salmon the traditional way. I wondered if when he visited her in the shed in order to be intimate he made her bathe first. When his grown son married another Indian woman from the river, did the captain approve?

Jane Johnson, who married the captain's son, proudly became a schoolteacher in the Chinook territory. Having received a formal education, she gladly accepted a teaching position. Her payment for a term spent teaching was a pig. White settlers paid her, an educated Native woman, with one pig that they delivered on the last day of the term and left tied up behind the schoolhouse. In this story passed down through my family over generations, the ending was always told in a light way, a humorous way, because when my ancestor came to collect her payment, all that remained was a partial carcass and a bit of rope. They laughed when they told the story of how a bear or a coyote had made off with Jane's salary. I found it less amusing. I was angry when I heard the woman was paid in livestock. Would they have paid a white man or woman with a farm animal? In old sepia-toned photos of Jane Johnson, she is dressed in white clothing and her hair is neat and tidy on her head. She is dressed like any white woman of her time, but still they saw through the conservative dress to the Indian beneath.

Jane's daughter was Myrtle Woodcock and was referred to by white settlers as the last Indian princess on account of the large celebration that happened on the day of her birth. Paddlers from different tribes all arrived on the banks of the river in their high-prow canoes and brought with them songs and gifts. A great feast took place to honor my ancestor, who was descended from Chief Hoquiam and Chief Uhlahnee. Myrtle Woodcock became a noted historian and

poet, publishing several poems in the Historical Society's quarterly magazine, *The Sou'wester.* In a black-
and-white photograph, Myrtle stands on a beach.
She's surrounded by an abundance of cedar woven
baskets and wears strings of beads. She's proud and
beautiful as she looks directly into the camera. In
a book of tribal stories put together by my great-
grandmother, I found one from Myrtle Woodcock.
She tells the story of the wild blackberry, how long
ago the berry was pale and bitter and not sought after
by the Native people. Until one day a young hunter
fell in love with a princess. But the princess was betrothed to a powerful chief in a neighboring tribe. On
the day of their wedding ceremony, the young hunter
was heartbroken and bitter and brought only a cedar
basket full of the tasteless wild berries as a gift. But
as the princess looked down at the berries, their color
became rich and deep, their aroma delicious. Their
desire for one another shined down onto the berries,
changing them into the deep sweet wild blackberries
they are today.

My ancestor's story resonated with me in the way
it seemed to embody her desire, her sexuality, her
identity as a Native woman. I wondered if she ever
had a forbidden love or if the white pioneers that she
mentioned in other poems and stories considered it
inappropriate for a young woman to tell such a story
in 1920.

I have wild blackberries tattooed on my body.

And though I've never been betrothed to or fallen in love with a hunter, I have been called wild. *Wild* is rooted in Myrtle's story. In her words I hear her challenge the patriarchy, the idea that we must always do what is expected of us. There is a fierceness in her story that courses through me.

"You're too wild for me." A lover actually said this to me once. When we started dating, I was a performer. I danced burlesque twice a week in Seattle and came straight from the club to our dates. I'd arrive in costume, in latex and lace. One morning we woke in his bed to smears of red glitter lipstick streaked like a gash across his bedspread. There were false lashes floating like black feathers around the sheets and a stray piece of weave curled along the floor like a pink serpent. We laughed at the grotesque display of my hyperfemininity littered across the room like a torn-apart doll, but I felt a creeping shame somewhere inside when I watched his face, his eyes on the pieces of me that had come apart beneath him. The idea of being too wild for him reached down into some deeper part of me. It was hard not to think of the woman who lived in the shed, in the dirt. It was hard not to remember the story of the pig or the wild blackberries.

I was too wild for a lot of people in my twenties. I wore my sexuality, my identity as queer person, as a high femme person, loud and proud. I was determined to take the parts of me that had been wounded and weaponize them. It was an act of reclamation. The memory of being assaulted by my boyfriend when I was seventeen had haunted me for years, and I was fighting against the shame he had instilled in me. I wanted to be strong and dangerous. I pushed things to the limits and vowed never to feel dirty or ashamed of my body again. This led to unsafe situations. Like the night a girlfriend and I sat in a park at dusk. It was a hot summer night and Capitol Hill was buzzing with club goers and crowds of people all searching for someone to take home. We had taken mushrooms and sat giggling on a mound of grass by a fountain. The sun sank beneath the skyline and the night sizzled with the hot black air of July. We drank a bottle of wine and watched the constellations blur and twinkle above us. A woman, much older than us with a green Mohawk, offered a six-pack of beer and joined us on our patch of grass. The mushrooms made my head spin, and as my girlfriend and the stranger sat cackling beside me I drifted off, feeling myself sink down into the soft green earth. When I came to, it was much later and my girlfriend and I were both in our underwear, heatedly making out on a small futon mattress. I had no idea how we had arrived at the woman's apartment, but when she came toward us with a vibrator, I shot up in a panic. My girlfriend and I hurried into our clothes and out the door. The sun was coming up as we dragged our tired bodies through downtown Seattle. People in suits pushed past us on their way to high-rise buildings and offices. They carried paper coffee cups and briefcases, and I saw several of them scowl at us as we made our way to the bus stop. When my girlfriend and I said good-bye before boarding the different buses that would take us home, she hugged me and we said things like "Yikes, that was a close call." We made light of it because we didn't know how else to hold it, whatever had just happened to us. Before she turned to board the bus, she picked a piece of grass from my tangled hair and laughed. "You're all dirty," she said.

To find partners with whom I feel safe enough to explore my sexuality without shame hasn't always been easy. Sometimes it's an experiment. Sometimes it's a moment of risk. I've looked for safety in unlikely places. But when I've found moments of that safe space in intimacy, it feels monumental. I have had partners project their idea of me, who they want me to be, onto me like an ill-fitting costume at times. I have had to learn ways not to get lost in their version of me. My body is the body of a Native woman. Like the ancestors who came before me no matter how I dress it up, what lies beneath is deeply indigenous.

Once while staying at my ex-husband's family cabin in the mountains, I explored what it meant to feel safely wild. We were alone and spent most of the night outside under the stars. We made out by a roaring bonfire. I remember the dirt beneath my finger-nails as I dug into the earth and straddled him. The heat from the fire blazed against our skin as I rocked against him. I stared up at the stars through the billowing smoke. The night felt wild and free and afterward we collapsed against each other and he grinned at me through the firelight. "I like you like this," he told me. "You're like some kind of feral witch." It felt empowering to be with him like that, in the night air with reckless abandon. But inside we fell asleep in the master bedroom. I woke to find I had bled on the sheets, leaving a big crimson stain blooming across the snowflake pattern of the flannel. Horrified, I rushed the sheets to the laundry room and washed the stain out the way my mother taught me, using hand soap and ice-cold water. I scrubbed my blood from the sheets and washed them twice. We made up the bed and tidied the cabin before leaving. A week later we received a scathing text from his mother. I had missed some smaller spots of blood, camouflaged in the patterns of snowflakes and pine trees. After that, every time we went to the cabin we were asked not to deal with the sheets, instead we were instructed only to strip the beds and leave the soiled sheets in the laundry room for his mother to handle herself. Every time we did this I was reminded of my stain, of how I had ruined the sheets. As a grown woman, a married woman, I'd wince in embarrassment as we took out the trash and recycling, as we dried the dishes and closed up the curtains and swept the floors but left the pile of sheets in the basket, unwashed and dirty.

I've returned to the river in moments of grief. When my marriage ended, the river called me back. I stripped naked in the cold rain and felt the damp sand between my toes. My skin was goose bumped in the frigid Northwest air and I watched my breath as it came like clouds from my lips. My feet sank into the mud as I inched out into the water. Then I let my body go. Beneath the surface I felt twigs and branches rush past. I felt all the river silt against my skin, and when I returned to shore shivering, I found wet leaves and silt clinging to me everywhere. I wrapped myself in a clean blanket and climbed back into the car leaving sand and dirt all over the upholstery.

There is more to the river than grief though. There is a memory of being on my great-grandmother's lap and smiling a big goofy grin, showing off a hole where a tooth had recently fallen out. My great-grandmother is smiling at me and holding the hood of her sweatshirt close to her face. The day is cold, but we're next to a big fire, and the sun peeks through the trees. My feet are caked in dirt and my shirt is speckled in stains. I'm happy.

Before I learned to dislike my body, and to distrust the bodies around it, the river was a place of joy. It was a place of strength and abundance. It was my ancestors' river, where they lived and fished. In my thirties I try to make sure I return to the river not only in moments of grief or when I am seeking to heal but also when I am happy. When I want to run along the beaches and feel the sand and the silt against my skin. I return to the river to remind myself where I come from and who came before me.

I brought the person I am in love with to the Nooksack River last summer. We pitched our tent right on the riverbank and spent our days hiking and swimming. I picked him thimbleberries and salmonberries. I picked him a fistful of wild blackberries and together we ate them and let the juices run down our chins and stain our fingertips a deep red. On our third night of not showering, the smell of campfire clung to our hair and permeated the tent. Our bodies smelled like the river, the wet grass, and the dirt. We laughed as we curled up together beneath the heavy blankets. He kissed me and I blushed. "But I'm so dirty," I laughed and teasingly pushed him away. He just wrapped his arms around me and buried his face in my neck. He kissed me there.

"I don't care," he said. And he brought his mouth to all the parts of me that I had ever been ashamed of. I felt his lips move across the landscape of my body in the dark of the tent and I felt how much he loved me, all of me.

The next morning, I watched my four-year-old niece as she ran wild along the riverbank, butt-naked through the tall meadow grass. When she wanted to show me her fairy house I grinned and followed her into a thicket. Inside she made us cakes, scooping heaps of river sand and mud into big piles at our feet.

She poured water over our cakes and packed them with her hands. I watched as she delicately placed the finishing touches on top: a salmonberry blossom, a couple of twigs, and one smooth stone from the river-bed. "They're beautiful," I said as we sat crouched in her fairy house. I accepted one big serving of muddy cake in my hands. My niece gave a proud nod of approval. We giggled at the mess we made. Our hands, our fingers, and our faces streaked and dirty.

That afternoon when the sun was at its highest and the air around us was thick with August heat, my niece was still naked and playing on the beach. She climbed up onto my lap and I read her a story from a big picture book, something about a water spirit, a fairy tale from Germany. Then I told her one of our tribe's legends, one my great-grandmother told me about the maiden who married the sea. Satisfied at the end of our story, my niece jumped off my lap and returned to running along the banks of the river. I joined my partner at the water's edge. "It's hot," he said, smiling. I nodded. Our skin was freckled in dirt and sweat and soot. We stripped down and dove into the icy water. Floating along the surface I listened to the sounds of the river, the rush and tumble of it. I heard my partner as he splashed and called my dog close, then the noise of my dog as she marched along the driftwood, the click-clacking of her claws back and forth as she trotted up and down the logs watching us. I could hear the breeze rustling in the giant cedar trees beyond the beach, and somewhere up the trail the sound of my cousin bringing an ax down on wood, chopping logs into kindling. Gentle waves moved over the pebbled beach and I loved the song of it all, but mostly I loved my niece's laughter as it floated over everything. Her laugh came from deep in her belly. I heard the sound of a girl full of joy and wildness, the laughter of a girl who knew at that moment that she was safe and loved.

Today my partner and I talked about our summer plans. We are planning a camping trip, a trip back to the river. And it isn't to grieve or mourn. It isn't to heal or cleanse things. It's to celebrate a recent teaching position I've accepted, one that pays an indigenous woman for her time with something other than livestock. We want to make sure we visit the river before classes start in the fall. We want to sleep under the stars and swim and pick berries. We want to feel the river silt beneath our feet and go to bed still dirty and smelling like campfire.

Black Cohosh

※

As a Native woman, I am wary of our country's health care system, of the conveyor-belt care we too often receive. In and out. *Here are your meds, there is the door.* We make jokes about the state of any given waiting room at any tribal health care clinic, the line of patients sometimes out the door, the peeling wallpaper, and out-of-date decor. My primary care physician isn't a person; it is a role, a revolving door of new faces because the doctors don't last long. Underpaid and overworked, they tend to disappear as often as the seasons change. Each time I go in for a checkup, we have to start at square one. I've learned to recite the patient intake questionnaire from memory. It's hard to imagine a time when our health and our bodies were tended to on our own terms, with our own medicine. In Coast Salish culture, we believe those who practice medicine have a sacred knowledge of plants, a connection to the earth and the creator. It's difficult to feel any connection to the way my ancestors might have practiced care when another young and ambitious new doctor walks into the room, carrying his clipboard and asking me routine questions about birth control and depression.

I know that I'll likely have to give this same practiced monologue again next time, to a brand-new doctor, but I stay because I don't have a choice. Due to insurance and the hierarchical, capitalist nature of our country's health care system, this is the option that is available to me.

There is a sign on the side of the highway that I drive by regularly. It challenges choice. In traffic jams on my way to the Seattle-Tacoma International Airport I am stuck staring at it. In my thirties I split my time between my ancestral home in the Pacific Northwest and my partner's home in Southern California. We are inching carefully toward a life together. Rather than either of us asking the other to give up their dreams, art, or community, we choose a split living situation. We never spend more than a month apart, and the road trips between our two homes are adventures in camping on the coast, roadside motels, and loud highway sing-alongs. My partner and I understand this is a luxury. I know I am able to do this because of the choices I have made. It's a privilege to be educated enough as a Native woman to be able to teach remotely, to be able to travel back and forth.

When I am back home in Tacoma, I pass by the billboard nearly every day. It's a twenty-foot portrait of a newborn baby's face. The photo looks ridiculously photoshopped, pink and glowing, a Precious Moments nightmare come to life. Beneath the obnoxiously white and cherublike child, the sign reminds us of the moment of conception. Another billboard has an equally pink and disturbingly massive baby's head and reads, THANKS MOM, FOR CHOOSING LIFE. I don't notice these signs as much when I'm in downtown San Diego or along the coastal highways of the fancy beach communities where my partner likes to surf. But I see them on the outskirts of the poorer neighborhoods. I see them near the reservation. I often drive by them and wonder why pro-life organizations feel more compelled to remind specific communities that we don't have a choice.

In my early twenties I was in an abusive relationship. Just barely twenty-one, I hadn't yet discovered my strength and lacked the ability to differentiate between love and abuse. I existed in a constant state of fear. I learned survival tactics and disillusion. I told lies to myself and the people who cared for me in order to validate choosing the relationship instead of my own safety. I didn't see the signs, and before I knew it, it was too late and I found myself hiding behind my locked bathroom door clutching my phone to my chest and ready to call 911 again if I had to. I'd sneak out of the window when he was too drunk, afraid to come home until morning. I forgave him every time. We broke up and got back together. I tried to leave. I even fell in love with someone else, Brandon, whom I'd eventually marry. But I'd find ways to sabotage it all in order to return to the man who locked me in rooms, who choked me, who threatened to kill himself if I ever walked out the door. Still I struggled to choose myself. It wasn't until his abuse reached beyond my own body and safety that I found the strength to leave. On a particularly bad night of his drinking, at an after-party, he assaulted one of our mutual friends. The moment escalated and he threw me to the ground in a blind rage. I hit the wood floor so hard I saw stars, and someone had to pull him off of me.

I left. It took the fear that I had enabled his behavior and put another woman in danger to finally choose myself and go. And I went hard. He moved out, and I swore to myself this would not end as it always had, in us getting back together. A month later I missed my period. I remember the exact moment I held the little plastic wand in my hand and wept. I didn't cry for what I knew was ahead of me. *Abortion* is a less frightening word for survivors. I cried because it had taken me so long to finally walk out the door, and the fear of depending on him for anything, financial assistance (I had no idea how much an abortion cost) or any kind of support, would threaten my chances of survival. I cried because I worried I was too weak to stay away, to choose myself over abuse.

When I held this little plastic wand, the positive result staring back at me, I looked instead to my forearm. I have a small circle burned above my wrist where he put a cigarette to my skin. I knew this pregnancy would leave a different kind of scar, something that would remind me of the nightmare I had survived or, worse yet, something that might keep me there. It threatened everything I had worked so hard for, the days I had managed to stay away. Making the decision was easy.

When Brandon, my new love, offered to support me if I wanted to keep it and go through with the pregnancy, I cried again. And not because I struggled with my decision. I knew immediately I had to have an abortion. I cried because no man had ever been that kind to me before. Feeling loved for real is a strange phenomenon when you've forgotten what it looks like. I was in shock. And I think this is an important detail to share, because even in the face of unwavering support, of the fact that if I had wanted to, I could have kept this pregnancy and had the emotional and financial support from someone who was safe, I declined. This is a luxury survivors are not often afforded, and still I chose myself. I wanted to do things. I was young, a waitress at a divey punk rock pizza joint and a burlesque performer. I hadn't seen anything beyond the reservation I grew up on or the city I moved to after. I hadn't accomplished anything other than staying alive in the aftermath of abuse and sexual assault. I wanted to do things. I wanted to travel, to go to school. I wanted to know what it felt like to be loved, to be happy and healthy.

Luckily, I was in the window of weeks that allowed me to get the abortion pill, and luckily Planned

Parenthood covered the cost. The only price for my abortion came in the form of an icy woman in a bad suit with a clipboard in a downtown Seattle office building before I was given the prescription. I shifted around uncomfortably in my chair as she prodded me with questions about my mental health. They made the psych evaluation sound mandatory. It was pre-abortion counseling, and had I known I had a choice, I would have refused the evaluation. I had not yet been diagnosed with PTSD, a diagnosis that would come later, and my body's response to being triggered was still a mystery. Her questions were ordinary and routine, but as I sat in the vinyl chair all I could think of were the different assaults I had survived. I began to shake and tremble. For whatever reason, talking to a complete stranger about my sexuality, my partners, and my history dislodged something in me, and I couldn't shake the feeling of hands tightly wrapped around my wrists or the weight of a man's body as it pushed into mine without consent. The woman made it clear that no matter what, I'd receive the pill, that was never in question, but she had no idea about my history of assault or the emotional impact her questions might have on me. I left angry and dizzy, face flushed, and on the verge of tears. I remember thinking in the elevator, *What the fuck was that about? And why was it necessary?*

I arrived home with the pharmacy bag containing the abortion pill and a heavy painkiller. I followed the instructions and took both medications as directed and waited. I woke up in a hospital bed. I had fallen in the bathroom and hit my head on the counter, and Brandon had rushed me to the ER. The painkillers had been too strong and I had a bad reaction. The doctors gave me a quick pelvic exam and sent me home, telling me to expect heavy bleeding over the next few days.

The bleeding was heavier than even the doctors had prepared me for, and I ignored my body's warning signs. I didn't want to talk about it. Weeks passed and I chose to suffer in silence, because when I thought about it, my mind went back to the woman and the clipboard, her sterile questions and cold gaze. The muscle memory of my trigger paralyzed me. When I thought about whatever was happening in my body, I couldn't separate it from the other abuses I had suffered. Weeks went by and I continued to bleed on everything. One night we got ready for a holiday party that I insisted on attending despite Brandon's hesitation. *You look pale*, he said. *I'm fine*, I responded. Hours into the party I stood in my cocktail dress picking at a fruit platter. All of a sudden, all the sound left the room. I focused on a stranger's mouth as it moved but I heard no words. I stumbled to the bathroom, losing consciousness the moment I shut the door. I woke up sweaty and dizzy, with my feet in cold metal stirrups in a hospital room. Brandon had discovered me in a cookie-sheet-size puddle of blood pooling beneath me on the tiled floor. He was at the hospital with my best friend. She was holding my hands, squeezing gently. *Don't look*, my friend whispered to me and she held my face in her hands. *Don't look*. She was crying, her face panicked, but trying to look calm.

The doctor told me the initial medication had not worked, not all the way. It had only half done the job. I remember the look on the young doctor's face when he asked, *Wait, you* did *have a pelvic exam?* The initial pelvic exam should have caught the problem, but it didn't. Instead I had been funneled in and out quickly, the way patients without good insurance are, and they failed to discover that my body had not completed the process, leaving dangerous matter in my uterus, which brought me close to septic shock. I remember the doctor shaking his head as he looked down at my chart, as he went over the dates I took the medication and had the pelvic exam. He let out a long sigh and told me, *You're lucky your friends brought you in here when they did* . . . His voice trailed off, but I knew what he meant. There was a silent understanding between us, and it filled the fluorescent room. The pelvic exam I'd had a month ago had not been thorough, and I had been in the hands of doctors who released me with barely a second glance and a prescription for painkillers. The infection would have killed me, maybe in a week, maybe in a couple of days.

You almost died, would have died. Part of me wanted the doctor to say it out loud, to bring into the room what wasn't being said. Because it was true: As a Native woman, a poor woman, a waitress without good insurance, I had been dismissed. Left for dead. I thought of all the other women who might have been funneled in and out, seen only as the information on their charts. Dollars and cents. Demographics. When it came to my survival, the choice I made for my own body, I had wished to be seen for what I was, an abuse and rape survivor, a young woman with her future ahead of her. Instead, I was seen only as the boxes I checked: No insurance. Native American. Seeking an abortion. And not being seen fully and carefully nearly killed me.

I think of my great-great-grandmother Louise Anderson, who as a young woman packed up her belongings, her medicines, and her daughter to go give care to a white woman who had come down with smallpox. She never stopped to consider the risk. It didn't occur to her, because why would it? She had the plant medicines necessary to bring down a fever, and she possessed the knowledge of how to heal. She saw the woman for what she was: not only white, not only a settler, but a human in pain. I wonder what the doctors who gave me that botched pelvic exam saw when they looked at me without even a fraction of the compassion my ancestor had for the stranger she tended to. Tattoos, twenty-one, waitress.

When I remember what I went through, what I survived, I still feel grateful for the choice that was available to me. That is a privilege. I was able to choose myself and my future, my chance at a healthy life. When I read the news that our Supreme Court had overturned *Roe v. Wade*, making safe abortions illegal, I felt afraid. Even in my home state of Washington the health care system had failed me, had almost killed me. I worry at the thought of young women seeking whatever alternative might be available to them if their state no longer offers safe and legal abortions. I think of the signs plastered around underserved communities, poor communities, the signs along the highway near the reservation I live on. Huge smiling infants in pastels and glowing light, reminding us of how fragile our right to choose is. It's hard not to get angry.

So I remind myself of a different story, the story a good friend shared with me. When a safe abortion was not available to her, when she found herself trapped and pregnant in not only an abusive relationship but a conservative state and conservative household, she turned to her old punk zines for help. One shared the recipe for a safe at-home abortion. The herbal remedy was detailed, with instructions on where to get the ingredients, how to make the tea, and what aftercare was necessary to heal properly.

My friend procured the ingredients in secret. She made the tea alone when everyone was sleeping. Her body did what it was supposed to and she had a safe recovery. She's far away from that relationship and has created a life for herself. She's healthy and happy.

My friend still has the zine that helped her safely perform and recover from an herbal abortion. She even showed me her own zine, something she created after her experience. *I just wanted to help*, she said, smiling. And as I delicately thumbed through her worn cut-and-pasted pages, I smiled too. I looked at my friend's work, how she had listed the ingredients, the steps to make the infusion, and even information pertaining to aftercare for your now nonpregnant body. I read over the passage detailing how to watch for tissue to make sure your body has safely passed the pregnancy and felt angry for my younger self. Why had no doctor told me that? So much care and attention had been put into her pages, and all because she wanted to *help*. I told my friend I wished I had known her back when I had made my choice, that perhaps I would not have had a brush with septic shock, with *death*. But holding her stapled zine in my hands brought a small comfort. It soothed the anxiety that has been inside my body ever since I discovered that my body was not always safe, even in the places you'd expect it to be, places like relationships, hospitals, and women's clinics. It soothed the anxiety that's reawakened by the fear that a safe and legal abortion might no longer be an option. But I heard my friend's gentle words, saw them on the page, in her statement *I just wanted to help,* and a calm washed over me.

Because information like this still exists. People are sharing the plant knowledge that, should it become necessary, will allow women to take matters into our own hands. It's hard not to think of my indigenous ancestors and their own plant medicines and how, before it was stripped away, they had everything they needed. There exists a deep and ancestral knowledge of how to take care of one another, and it was there long before the imposition of a health care system that continues to fail.

Now when I pass by that sign on the highway, the one that tries to play on my emotions while simultaneously threatening to remove my agency, my choice, I scoff at it and keep driving. I look up at that angelic, fat, white baby smiling down at me and I smile back. I remember the stories that are being shared and the plant knowledge and medicines that have been in use by indigenous communities long before we needed legislation and rulings. I smile because we have everything we need.

The main ingredient in an herbal abortion is black cohosh.

ʔuʔušəbicid čəd

An Indigenous Queer Love Story

During a fight, my ex-husband told me that I had learned how to love the wrong way. My family, he had said, gave me a bad example of love. When he told me this, all I could think of were the things I did or did not learn from the parents who raised me. I didn't learn how to change my own oil. I did learn about our tribe's salmon ceremony. I didn't learn how to quietly have an argument. I did learn about our traditional language. I didn't learn to make elaborate baked goods. I did learn how to bake salmon over a piece of soaked cedar. I didn't learn the expected things, the basic things, like how to fold a fitted sheet, or drive a car, or play the piano. I left home at fourteen. I didn't learn a lot of the things my friends who came from different kinds of families might have. And apparently I had learned how to love the wrong way.

When he said it to me it tore my brain in half, shredded it up, left me blank. I had loved him, had been so undeniably in love with him, for nearly a decade of my life. It was one of those sickeningly perfect fairy-tale loves too. For ten years in our twenties we had what most people wanted: fiery passion, adventurous road trips, European tours with bands, all against a backdrop of a home, a life we were building. It ended. We both played our roles in that. I wrote a book about it. But I was stuck on the assessment he had made. I couldn't move past it. Couldn't stop digging at it. Had I learned how to love wrong? This assessment, born out of frustration and heartache, attacked something deeper. It attacked my family, where I come from. It attacked my indigeneity.

Love historically does not bode well for the women I come from. For over five generations the women of my lineage have been monumentally fucked over by *love*. Love has been weaponized against us in varying degrees of violence and abandonment. In cases of ownership and gain, love has been used to defeat us as indigenous women and like pipelines and dams has been instrumental in draining our resources, in depleting our power.

Love, like so many things, has been a tool in our undoing.

A brief timeline of love as historical markers for the women in my family:

- In 1828, ships from the Hudson's Bay Company arrive in my ancestor Comptia Koholowish's Chinook territory, bringing with them the European disease smallpox that decimates her entire village. She later marries one of the Scottish sea captains who arrived on these ships, becoming Mrs. James Johnson. She is mother to his children, but because of her *Indian* status is forced to live out her life in a shack on the edge of *his* property line. She is never allowed in the main house.

- In the 1930s, my great-grandmother is married twice and divorced. She buries her baby in Quinault after he dies of meningitis at age three.

- In 1945, my great-grandmother marries a white man, a war hero who adopts her children as his own and builds her a home in South Seattle. Before his death he admits to still loving his first wife, a white woman, and makes a pilgrimage to visit his estranged first love after years of marriage to my great-grandmother.

- In the 1950s, my grandmother marries a man who works for the Indian Health Service and gives birth to my mother and uncle. They divorce shortly thereafter and my grandmother suffers through a string of failed relationships, admitting to this day she is still not over my grandfather.

- In the 1970s, my mother meets my biological white father and has a mock wedding at age fourteen with silver rings. She becomes pregnant with me at nineteen. He abandons her before I am born. I have one photo of him, and my mother's teenage wedding ring.

- By age nineteen, I have already survived the first

of two abusive relationships, one ending in abortion and an attempted restraining order.

- In my twenties, I fall in love with a woman whom I allow to do things with my body I have never done since. The woman breaks up with me the next day.

- By age thirty, I have found my Agent Cooper and marry him in a traditional Coast Salish wedding ceremony. On the day of our wedding he is withholding and leaves me for a band tour using our honeymoon money to buy his plane ticket. We divorce a year later.

My first consensual sexual experiences were with the girls I loved when I was a teenager. I think back and remember feeling ablaze in it, the fire and the heat of it, burning with teenage hormonal desire, but there was also a sense of safety in it, something I hadn't known. At a party when I was fifteen, I crawled into bed with a girlfriend and the first boy I loved, a boy who also had the gift of making me feel safe. The three of us drifted off to sleep in the early hours of the morning and I remember wanting this, wanting the three of us to stay curled up and warm together for eternity, because to me the moment felt perfect. Years later, that first boyfriend revealed to me the immense sense of dread and anxiety he had felt that entire night, how he hadn't slept a wink, how he lay there alone with the sounds of our breath, staring at a poster of PJ Harvey on the ceiling, worried he had lost me. "I can't listen to PJ Harvey and not think of that night," he told me. I think of the part he said about losing me. To lose me suggests he had me, had a claim to me; it implies ownership.

Later, as an adult, I remember a date asking me one night, as we sat by her fire, what percentage of me loved women and what percentage loved men. I understand now that perhaps she had worded the question wrong, that perhaps hers was a question more site specific, one specifically about my love for her and my love for the other person I was seeing. The other felt too binary, like an equation. It wasn't a question I had an answer for and still don't. The question poked at a bruise in me, poked at my identity, my sexuality. I never thought of it that way. I never tried to gauge my attraction to gender. I felt in between something.

I have tried and failed repeatedly to cultivate a partnership that feels right to me. I have been honest and forthcoming. One man asked me shortly into our relationship, *Are you gay?* I shrugged. *No, but I suppose I'm not straight either.* This confused him. He needed a framework. He needed titles. He wanted to know. I offered. He laughed at this, making jokes about an ex-girlfriend in college going through a phase. *It was pretty hot*, he added. That relationship was short lived.

When I fell in love with Marguerite, my husband at the time was annoyed. I guess that's fair. But try as

I might, I couldn't convince him that my heart had space enough for the both of them. Marguerite and I went on dates and on wild road trips down the coast. She and I were inseparable, but I always came home. Every night. She had been a third in a relationship before, and mostly our situation worked. I felt for a time that my queerness was seen and respected. I tried to compartmentalize. If *throuple* is the right word, let's use that here. It's what I wanted, what I craved. The three of us shared intimacy on occasion, but it was rigid. It existed under a blanket of rules. I tried to adhere to the hierarchies of my relationship, but it was hard to do when one person, my ex-husband, so clearly wanted the relationship to fit to his mold. His idea of who I was binary. It was the me that existed when we were alone, and the me that existed when Marguerite was over. They were held separate, never seen as a whole and never wholly accepted. In a passionate argument he hit me with that statement that I had learned to love the wrong way. Meaning that the way my heart craved both his and Marguerite's affection was inherently wrong. This tore me in half. It divided me and left me floating, two scraps of a page falling delicately toward a floor.

Your family gave you a bad example of love, he had said. And the statement left me lonely, left me orphaned and lost. Because when my mother remarried a Coast Salish man, the man who would stick around and raise me, the man who would love me, scold me, ground me, and be an actual father to me, I felt lucky. I had been given the gift of a father in a man who deeply loved my mother, who would never abandon her despite the many opportunities he may have had to do so. I had been loved. And so had she. She had been out and open about who she was, and the man who became my father accepted all of her. This was my first example of love.

Pre-contact and pre-Christianity, my ancestors were believed to have practiced a lifestyle that granted them multiple partners. Claudia lived with us, my mom, dad, siblings, and me, when I was eleven. I learned things from Claudia. She drove a small blue pickup truck, loved the Cranberries, and also loved my mom. My mom loved Claudia too. Claudia taught me how to throw and catch a baseball and how to be tough when a pet died. Once on a family outing to the movies, Claudia and I were in the public restroom and when a girl and her mother mistook Claudia, with her butch presentation, for a man, they accused us of being in the wrong restroom. I looked at Claudia, in her blue Levi's, white T-shirt with the sleeves rolled up, and slicked-back hair, and saw the woman who loved my mother. That day Claudia taught me how to be strong while still being polite. I loved her like a second mother, because for a time that's what she was. Claudia didn't sleep on the couch, and there were no guest rooms in our single-wide trailer on the reservation. Claudia, each night with my parents, retreated to the parent bedroom. This never felt like a deficiency. In fact, it felt like quite the opposite. Instead of two adults around, for a time my family had three.

The love lesson here is layered. It exists in a stack of compassion. Care for my mother from my father, care for Claudia from my mother, and care for both of them from Claudia. The thing is, it worked. And no one felt slighted, or abandoned, or unfulfilled. At least for a time. Even straight relationships are complex and not without their problems. Heteronormative relationships exist from the beginning with the things that will eventually end them. If an end is the outcome. There was an ending to my mother and Claudia's relationship but not an ending to their love. The two women have remained close for over twenty years. My mother went kayaking with Claudia on the last hot day of this summer. Claudia attended a reading I did at the University of Washington last year, and seeing her felt like seeing a parent who no longer lives with me. So what about this is *wrong*?

I struggle still with the assessment my ex made. I second-guess myself. I wonder if I'll ever be able to make a partner happy, knowing there will always be two divided parts of me. Two twins occupying the same heart.

The first time I ever heard the term *Two Spirit* I felt a sense of relief wash over me. My mother had just come back from the Two Spirit gathering in Montana. As we pored over photos of her and my dad amid the celebration, I was thrilled to see all those indigenous queer folks in one place. I saw my mom posing with the most beautiful drag queens in their regalia. I saw wing dresses and glitter makeup and my dad at the DJ booth. I saw a place where everyone seemed to be safe and smiling. It made sense to me. For as long as I could remember, I had felt two opposite poles tugging somewhere inside me. I felt pulled in different directions, conflicted, constantly indecisive. *Two Spirit* is how many Native communities refer to indigenous queer identity. When it was explained to me, it translated simply to someone with both a masculine and a feminine spirit, someone who exists between gender, someone who is capable of loving regardless of Eurocentric, heteronormative binaries. This new definition quelled a lifelong anxiety, something that had taken root in me early on.

When I told a Native friend about the ways I struggled with my ex's assessment that I had learned to love the wrong way, she scoffed. She rolled her eyes and shook her head. Then she showed me a short film. The film is only a few minutes long, and in those short minutes the screen tells the story of three characters. It is easy to piece together that the three people are in love and existing as a family. They are dressed in the traditional way. They are all indigenous. Though there is little dialogue, the imagery suggests a story about love that existed before the arrival of European settlers, a time before missionaries and churches, a time before the concepts of love and family were warped by Eurocentric ideals of purity and control. I was in tears by the time the credits rolled. I had never considered this story before. Instead, I had listened to the ways people told me I was wrong, that my kind of love was wrong.

It took a long time before I could tell my current partner I loved him. This was born out of fear. The fear of rejection, misunderstanding, and abandonment drove me to bite my tongue every time I felt the words close to spilling from my lips. I didn't want to be wrong again. I didn't want to be invisible or erased. I wanted to say the words true and have them fall on ears that listened and truly heard them.

Blaine and I had been dating long-distance for a while when I met Kari. She responded to a post some friends and I had made looking for a drummer. She came walking down the street, her teal hair falling past her shoulders over her Realtree camo jacket, carrying her snare drum. As we played through the songs, I'd trip up, getting lost in the lyrics, and was monumentally bad at keeping time. Kari's eyes would flash into mine and we'd grin and look away. When

I'd get lost I'd look to her, and she'd bring me back with a smile and a nod. Our chemistry was instant. Like me, she also had a long-distance love, and we bonded over fantasy novels and pop music. Our first date was at Cinerama, where we ate too much chocolate popcorn and talked shit about J. K. Rowling.

I paced nervously on the phone. I worried about all the things that had happened in my past. I worried about disappointing him, I worried I was loving him the wrong way. To my surprise he was gentle and understanding. He related to me, telling me of his own queer identity, how he had crushes on different people regardless of gender. I felt my whole body sigh with relief. Being able to relate in our queer identity only brought us closer together, and everything got better. Our intimacy, our words, the way we held and saw each other felt effortless. He told me his first crush, RuPaul, manifested itself in the nineties. As a teenager, he had thought she was the sexiest thing he had ever seen. *When my brother told me that RuPaul was actually a man,* he confided, *I didn't care. Because what does gender have to do with desire?* I knew again that I loved this person, felt akin to his heart. But still, I could not say the words.

When the band Kari and I were in played a punk fest that Blaine puts on in San Diego, I was nervous. I worried about all the things that had plagued my last situation, in which I found not one but two spaces occupied in my heart. But my concerns were unfounded. I loved them both in different ways. I loved the way Blaine was warm and kind and open, unthreatened because there was no threat. There was an understanding, a transparency. Kari had a partner whom she loved and had a commitment to. Blaine and I also had a deep love and unwavering commitment to each other. And Kari and I still had our love; though it existed within the parameters we had laid, it was there. Later we would take Kari to the airport, where we would say goodbye and she would fly home. Blaine and I would settle next to the fire and sip cocktails and relish a night alone after a long weekend of crowds. We would stay up late and love each other with words and touch, feeling closer than ever.

I think of the term *Two Spirit*. I had spent so much of my life wrestling the two halves of me into submission, to be better, to be someone worthy of love. I never imagined a different version, a version in which I did not have to choose. In some cultures, Two Spirit people are regarded as sacred, as those in the tribe closest to the spirit world, and they are celebrated. It isn't a burden to be different, it's a gift, and the shame I've learned to carry is the work of generations of colonization. I spent a long time wondering what it meant to learn how to love the wrong way. And I think I understand now that the biggest mistake I ever made was trying to pretend to be something I'm not, to not have compassion for myself, to not love myself. The deepest wrong I had known was not in what I did to others but in what I didn't allow myself to do, to embrace all the parts of me in order to be whole. *Whole.* There's that word again. Even the way I've struggled to identify as something *whole*, something I've desired most of my life, is a colonial construct, one that implies that the *two* within me need to separate or assimilate. Because how could I possibly love from a divided place, a place that celebrates the duality within me?

The day I decided to tell Blaine that I loved him, I walked with my mom on the trails along Swan Creek. She was wearing a T-shirt with a Lushootseed phrase printed across the front, *ʔuʔušəbicid čəd.* I asked her what it meant and as she began to explain, I interjected. *So, it means* I love you? I asked. But my mom corrected me, she said it meant more than that. It wasn't a romantic love, she explained, but a deeper love. It meant *I have unconditional love for you, I have compassion for you.* I felt a weight lift from my heart, one I had been carrying for so many years. The phrase made sense to me. It unpacked and undid all the expectations that I had put on lovers and partners and the expectations they had put on me. I did love Blaine in a romantic way, of course, but this phrase spoke of a love that transcended that, a love that reached beyond want and desire. This love was about compassion.

I practiced the phrase over and over, trying to get the pronunciation right. And when Blaine and I finally did say *I love you*, I told him in Lushootseed. It was important for me to say it, not only to speak in my traditional language but also because of the distinction between the two phrases. One feels like a colonized love and is in itself an act of colonization, to desire someone, to want them, to try to own part of them. The other feels like a love that is open and without boundaries or ownership. It felt safer to me.

I say *I love you* to my partner in the traditional way, in a way that reaches beyond the colonizer's language. I do this in memory of my ancestors and all the ways they had to fight for their kind of love. A love that comes without resources and ownership. A love that reminds us we are worthy of care and affection, no matter the container. When missionaries and colonizers arrived in my ancestors' land, they taught them that only one way to love was acceptable. They bent and broke us to their will. They tried to erase a deeper concept of love, one that nurtures our whole hearts. My partner wanted to know, *Are you polyamorous?* Meaning, *Do you require multiple partners at once?* The answer is no. But I do need the freedom to embrace my queer heart, to accept and celebrate it and let it run wild through the relationship. I speak the Lushootseed words to him to remind myself that the ways I've learned to love are not and have never been wrong. I say *ʔuʔušəbicid čəd* and there is no

English phrase that can carry all its meaning. It isn't simply a romantic love, or love based in desire, or a fairy-tale ending. It's a love that extends to compassion and care. It is an act of radical decolonization, the freeing of my own heart. It's my own happily ever after, a beginning and an ending. It's my indigenous queer love story.

Si?aλ̓: Orations: 5

※

Today is fair. Tomorrow it may be overcast with clouds.*

Chief Seattle stood before settlers over a hundred fifty years ago and spoke; some say he surrendered. I believe differently. I believe because I have to, because it is necessary in order to move through the world as the ancestor of a colonized people. I believe that in that speech he was still strategizing. He was trying to tell his people they were outnumbered. *Outnumbered* isn't over, isn't hopeless. *Outnumbered* just means the world as they knew it was changing. Perhaps he believed if he could change with it, there would be a chance of survival.

When the Coast Salish territory was settled and when the city began to finally take shape, entire ecosystems were changed. Tideflats were buried over. Natural marshes and waterways were filled in with dirt in order to make the land inhabitable. My ancestors lost their food supplies, the places they harvested shellfish, and their homes. When I walk the streets of Seattle, I have learned to fight the feelings of shame that creep up in me. How I once craved the white things this place had to offer me: grunge, punk rock, art, and music, the fantasy of a life I never believed was meant for me, an Indian, a descendant of the defeated. I think of my daydreams, all those years spent enamored with the things that made this city everything it became but left nothing of what it once was. This land was sacred. It held spirits and memories. Battles, victories, and moments of joy, of love, of everything dear to its original inhabitants. There was beauty and abundance here and a thriving people. This is the source of pride I recognize now. Now when I walk the streets of Seattle, past Pike Place Market, flower stands, Elliott Bay, past record shops and music venues and the Amazon headquarters, I understand that the pavement beneath my feet tried to erase that history. My history.

This is a cautionary tale. One that asks, *Can we change things? Can we survive?* Chief Seattle welcomed his oppressors because he had to. Because he tried to see a better outcome for his people. He cared about the well-being of his tribe, he cared about survival enough to welcome change. Even if that change meant the inevitability of an oncoming storm. *Today is fair. Tomorrow it may be overcast with clouds.* And it *was* overcast with clouds, and a storm did come to the Coast Salish territory in a hurricane of settlers, of industrialization, of epidemics and erasure. We're here again. Face-to-face with impossible threats, the climate crisis, the world strangled in the chokehold of late-stage capitalism. Houseless populations have reached record highs. There are book burnings in certain states, the continuing murder of black and brown bodies, of trans bodies. People get killed in clubs for no reason. Women in some parts of the country are looking up home abortion recipes. The oceans are becoming acidic. The planet is dying.

In 1854 Chief Seattle was considering his future, the future of his people. One hundred and fifty years later, my great-grandmother was doing the same. She was considering the fate of her people, of the entire world. This isn't a coincidence. There is something inherently radical, inherently hopeful, that is hardwired within Coast Salish ways of thinking. I've grown up with these stories and these teachings. If I understand at least part of the lesson, I know it has to do with compassion, with care for the natural world and for one another. There is something to learn from indigenous ways of thinking that has to do with courage and resilience, because even in the face of attempted genocide, of erasure, we descendants are still here.

Over the past several years I have attended many protests. I have listened to the speeches and the songs. To me, the message remains the same. There are forces of oppression, of greed, that wish to erase us. If we don't consider change, what future will we have?

When my great-grandmother handed the composer the tape that held Chief Seattle's voice, she was asking the whole world to listen. She was asking us to consider something better, something stronger.

I am asking the same thing. Are you listening yet?

Kinships

※

PART ONE: HABOO

Kinship, noun: blood relationships
similar : sharing of characteristics or origins

Gecko Hawai'i

My great-grandmother brought me a gift once when I was still small enough to climb into her lap and paw at her glasses like an animal. I was like that. I was needy. Always hungry and clawing. Applauding her every syllable. She was a storyteller and this made her godly. When other kids played, I stayed in, laid out at her feet, body yawning like a cat; I was listening. You'd think this meant I was a good kid, but my attention was self-serving. You see, I was afraid of ever missing anything she might say. We were taught traditionally to say *haboo* at the end of a story; this was to show you were listening. But every time I clapped, it was *haboo, another story, haboo, keep talking, haboo, never leave me.* When my great-grandmother went to Hawai'i, I was awash with grief and curiosity. She was working on language, on preservation, because something I hadn't even been aware of was disappearing. She brought back photos of landscapes lush and green and had seen inside volcanos, the earth cracked open and burning. I bit my tongue, wrung with worry, that she might again leave me. I was selfish that way. The day she brought me the foam gecko on a wire, she had to show me how it worked. I didn't get it at first; I've always been a slow learner. But when the neon green thing began to dance and follow her, I was enchanted, spellbound by my great-grandmother, who had found even more magic. For days the gecko shadowed me. We trampled the house, the sidewalk, the yard, parading. But when it started to disintegrate, leaving parts of its dismembered body all over the carpet, I picked them up one by one and held them together with tape, but soon it was too late, and all that remained was the wire, clinging to a soft chunk of its face. It thudded on the ground behind me in a tragic display. I didn't know at the time that I was mourning. So I crawled into my great-grandmother's lap wailing. Begging her to bring him back to me, to save anything from ever disappearing. And she hushed me as I cried, as I tried to be brave. She smiled and rocked me gently as I repeated the only traditional word I knew. *Haboo. Haboo. Haboo.* Another story.

This was one of Vi's favorite places. Grandma Vi's friend placed another grainy photograph down on the mosaic of snapshots we had been building across the tabletop after dinner. It's been ten years since the story of our great-grandmother changed, since it became a grief story. A story about missing something. A story about loss. I looked down at the photo. Grandma, black blouse, amber skirt against volcanic rock, beads of coral around her neck, arms up, smiling as a wave crashed beyond her small frame, leaving her haloed in white water. *Here's another.* The woman, who was more like family and less like one of Grandma's language students, laid the photo down. I looked at our great-grandmother, locked in some moment in the early nineties. She was still smiling, her arm outstretched over a pond as she scattered bread crumbs, ducks circling for the feeding frenzy. This was my great-grandmother an ocean away. This was her, the visual evidence of her. Before, all I could do was imagine.

When I was small, I imagined her there, across the ocean, on the island of Hawai'i. She would bring me and my cousins little gifts, proof that she had stood on volcanoes, swum in warm oceans, and visited ancient places. Ancient places that had nothing to do with us, our lineage, our Coast Salish history. But she returned again and again. She made the same trip over the years, despite my great-grandfather refusing to accompany her. He couldn't go back. He carried the weight of Pearl Harbor on his shoulders. He was haunted by the Moananuiākea, the vast Pacific. So year after year Grandma returned alone or accompanied by a friend, like the friend who sat with me over dinner sharing old photographs of Grandma's favorite places on the island. It felt like a key to a door, a key that had long gone missing. I knew that she had gone almost every year. I knew that it had something to do with the university, with her language work. In the photos she is full of joy, she's in awe of everything around her. She's caught mid-laugh with a Hawaiian woman on the side of a lava desert. *That was a dear friend of Vi's*, she tells me. And suddenly I am wracked with grief. I am missing the woman who named me, who helped raise me, who bestowed on me such a weight. When my great-grandmother's friend said goodbye to me that night, she sent me off with some photos and a map of the Big Island. On it she had marked beaches and trails, the university in Hilo, the City of Refuge, and an old Japanese restaurant where Grandma went whenever she was working on that side of the island. *She loved to feed the ducks there*, Grandma's friend was warm when she told me, lost in some memory of Miyo's and the duck pond there. I thanked her as we embraced and said goodbye. She told me to have a good trip, and I was grateful for her time, for these photos and places laid out like a treasure map, one that I believed held the key to getting back to her, my namesake, our great-grandmother.

This would be my second trip to the Big Island. I had been reluctant to make the first journey the previous year. I felt uncomfortable traveling to an island so recently impacted by the forces of colonization. *What right do I have to be here?* I asked my partner when he presented me with the invitation. When I saw the reports of the impact of tourism, the masses of well-to-do white families that crashed the small communities like tidal waves and ravaged the resources, I couldn't reconcile the guilt I felt, couldn't explain it to my white partner, who had been raised there. When I finally agreed to go, I felt ashamed. As a Native woman it's sometimes hard for me to take up space in places that remind me so blatantly of our history.

That first trip to the Big Island was short, just a few days between work to meet his family and see where he grew up. What I remember most is stepping off the plane into the open air of the Kona airport. I closed my eyes and felt an unexpected wave of familiarity wash over me. Something about the floral sweet air, the hot asphalt beneath my feet, the sunlight as it poured in over the old luggage carousel, the soft whirring metal noise as it turned, all of it felt like someplace I had been before.

This happens sometimes. A memory that doesn't feel like mine saturates my senses and I usually call my mother. I knew that Grandma had come to Hawai'i throughout my life, but I didn't know the details, on which islands she had spent the most time. When my mom picked up the phone she laughed gently, *No, it wasn't just déjà vu*, she said. No, I wasn't crazy. The Big Island *was* the island Grandma came to the most. It was where she did the most language work, where she grew friendships, where she returned to again and again. This was her favorite island. I hadn't known that. This new information led me to seek out our family friend when I returned home. I had questions. I had felt my great-grandmother's presence so strongly in that airport, and across the winding roads that led us away from town along the coastline, and even deep in South Kona where my partner grew up. I knew that before I went back to that place I would have to get more of the story.

When I spent the evening with my great-grandmother's friend, she told stories of their shared adventures. It felt like time traveling, like I could somehow reach her in these places that meant so much to her. And so, a year later, with my new stack of photos and the twenty-year-old map tucked under my arm, I returned to the Big Island, excited by the opportunity to retrace my great-grandmother's footsteps.

I was comforted by the places I knew she had stood. I followed the same trails she had walked, and every time I left a coil of hair in the dirt or the sand, I was speaking to her. I became quite emotional and some days I'd spend the long car rides across the island quiet, enveloped in memory, in language and story. As my partner made the long treks from Honokaʻa to Waimea, I'd rest my head on the window, staring out at the street names as they passed by. Almost every street in Hawai'i is written in the traditional language, the towns and the highways too. I began to understand what brought my great-grandmother back every year. Here is a place where on any given radio station you can hear the traditional language. You see it on signs, in storefronts. It's loud and powerful, reverberating across the island like a song. And she could hear it. I think she felt inspired by it, like some part of her knew she had to give her own language a fighting chance.

Back on the continent, traditional languages are less known, buried by years of cultural erasure and colonization. When she was young, Grandma began to notice that the last fluent elders of her tribe were passing, and with them our language was on the brink of extinction. I often wondered how she became so tenacious, so bold in her mission to keep our Lushootseed language in this world. How she transcribed and created a written language has always been so mesmerizing to me. When I think of her in the 1970s and '80s, already a grandmother, I often wondered how she found the determination to keep going, even in the face of colonialism, racism, and forces that wished to silence her. On those long drives across Hawai'i, it became obvious to me that coming here guided her, pushed her forward. Perhaps it was here that she found the strength and the will to not let our own language fade into silence.

One photo of my great-grandmother in Hawai'i is of her and a friend I didn't know. Her smile is big and radiant as she stands mid-laugh next to a Hawaiian woman. I know from her language student that this woman, Pualani Kanaka'ole Kanahele, had a profound impact on my great-grandmother, that the two were both storytellers and language teachers and remained friends over the years. When they met, they were already grandmothers, and looking at the photo, the two could be sisters. I have wondered about the possibility of seeking out the descendants of my great-grandmother's friend, to ask them questions, to see if they remember. Something about this friendship moved me, how it spanned oceans and decades. How in each other the two women found a kindred spirit, formed a connection, a kinship.

PART TWO: CANOE JOURNEY

Canoe, noun: a light, narrow boat, propelled by paddling

On my most recent trip to the Big Island I sat on a beach while my partner surfed. He had left me a snorkel mask and encouraged me to swim out along the reef if I got too hot, saying there were most likely sea turtles out at this time of day. Instead, I sat in the blistering heat, notebook in my lap, as I filled its pages with poetry. I wrote about the small blue church ahead of me and how it seemed out of place at the water's edge. I wrote about the duck pond at Miyo's, about how when no one was looking I leaned the weight of my body against a coconut tree and cried. About how my friends chatted somewhere behind me, how I stood on the sponge-soft grass along the pond, directly where my great-grandmother had once stood, content and smiling as she tossed bread. I looked at the ducks circling. Granddaughter ducks. Maybe. I wrote it all down. How my partner had taken me on Grandma's tour of the island twice now. How I think I fell in love with him more each day. With every story he told—how he learned Hawaiian words in kindergarten, how he understood at a young age he was a guest on this island—I relaxed the wall I had learned to construct around my heart, specifically around white men, who have the capacity to vanish things. He told me stories of schoolyard fights and how he learned to be quiet, how to behave on land that doesn't belong to you. *You'd get pounded for that*, he'd say about boys in his grade who came from California and tried to take up too much space.

Posted up on the beach as he surfed, I felt grateful for him. I was grateful for the quiet, the solitude. He knew the stories that looped in my head and he knew how badly I needed to write them down. I wrote poems for my great-grandmother, for my ancestors. I wrote poems about Land Back, decolonization, and cultural revitalization. I wrote a poem about salmon for my friend Tayi because the sun and the beach made me miss her.

Tayi and I met when she was visiting from New Zealand. She was on her West Coast book tour and stayed with me at my home in Tacoma. We had done several book festivals and readings together. And in her I had found a kindred spirit. Together we showed up at author after-parties feeling out of place. We showed up in lace and latex, in boots and lip gloss, hovering over the snacks, wondering if it was just us or were the other writers not talking to us? *Maybe they're just scared of us, indigenous women, indigenous women writers,* and we laughed and filled our plates with fish and drank free Chardonnay before taking a Lyft to the punk club. We did oyster shooters in Port Townsend and when I showed her a Coast Salish carving, she whipped around to show me the back of her sweatshirt, adorned in Māori art. *Look at the similarities.* And we both smiled, because of course there were similarities.

On her last week in the Pacific Northwest, Tayi visited my class at the Native Pathways program at Evergreen State College. The students lit up in her presence, ignited by her laugh, her words, and the simple way she spoke truths about indigeneity, trauma, and resilience. Out on the stairwell we both took puffs off our nicotine vapes after class. It's exhausting being inspiring, being strong. As we puffed clouds of strawberry and mango out into the Northwest drizzle, Tayi broke the quiet rhythm of inhale/exhale. *What is that?* she asked and her head tilted toward a large wooden structure ahead of us. I admitted I didn't know. *It looks Māori,* she responded. So together we trekked in the rain down the stairs and up to the building.

The weaving studio was a collaboration between two Native artists. One was Coast Salish, the other Māori. We approached the building exchanging glances. The woodwork that adorned the structure was half her culture and half mine. There were figures in the wood. It was hard to distinguish the different styles, the overlap in our tribes' aesthetics. We circled the studio in opposite directions, eyeing the story carved in both Māori and Lushootseed. Even the figures of the pillars shared the same abalone eyes. We met in the middle. *It's us,* my friend exclaimed, *this building is* us. And as we embraced, we laughed. We wiped tears from our eyes.

That same week we were invited to a screening of a documentary. *Salmon People* was a film made by Native activists and followed the story of Coast Salish people's fight to save our rivers and waterways, to save our salmon. Tayi and I spent the evening thronged in passionate conversation. We spoke excitedly about the different ways indigenous activism and cultural revitalization were taking shape, even in our own communities that seemed worlds apart, separated by oceans, yet remained so intrinsically connected.

The day after the documentary Tayi and I walked with a friend in Swan Creek. She wanted to see the forest, the woods that were so much a part of me. We walked altered. We had ingested a small amount of hallucinogenic mushrooms, with care and intention, to lift the veil if we could. We wanted to commune with our ancestors. On the trails we both noticed the same faces in the trees and climbed the same log that stretched over the creek because we thought we had seen something. We talked about the salmon returning, how that documentary had given us hope. Then, before leaving the woods that day, as we stepped carefully across the stream bed, we saw it there. We both looked immediately up at each other: Were we really seeing this? Was this here? In the dry creek bed, along the stones, like it had just unearthed itself, was the smallest fish I had ever seen. We screamed when we realized what it was, a perfectly intact fish, not rotten or bloodied or hooked. Its scales rainbowing silver in the daylight. What was it doing here? How did it get here? We puzzled over the logic as we made our way up the trail. When we reached my house, we both googled it. That small fish was a salmon. We had talked about spirits and ancestors throughout the hike. We had talked about them bringing us together. We had wanted proof that, as their descendants, as their granddaughters, we would see change in our lifetime. The salmon appeared to us, and for a moment I wasn't sure it was real. I questioned it. But days later I walked the trail alone. The fish was there, still fresh and silver.

On her last day, I took Tayi to my uncle's carving studio. He was restoring a canoe, in preparation for the annual Canoe Journey. Together we climbed into the boat. She told me how her ancestors also traveled by canoe, how they were carvers. *We both come from water people*, she told me. And in the canoe, we felt a kinship. My uncle shouted *paddles up*, and we held them high. We smiled as he snapped a photo. We talked about the meaning of the Canoe Journey, how different tribes come together and paddle. This is a Coast Salish tradition, one that happens every year. It's about togetherness, community, and strength. Tayi and I both got emotional when we said goodbye that day. We hugged hard and long and cried. I hadn't realized how much I needed a friend like that, another new writer, someone who understood, who felt worried for the world and worried for our indigenous communities. And I begged her to come back in the summer, to come to Canoe Journey with me.

Like the unexplainable salmon in the dry creek bed, another strangely magical thing happened a week after Tayi left. Another writer, one whom I recently had the privilege of interviewing for a lecture series, called me out of the blue. Julian is an indigenous human rights lawyer, an environmental rights lawyer, and of the Chamorro people, the indigenous people of Guam. The two of us met briefly and formed an immediate kinship. He was writing a review of Tayi's book. How incredible, he had remarked when we first met, that she would be staying with me, that he was working on her review. What are the odds? And we both laughed. Small world. Small indigenous writer world.

Julian had called out of the blue to ask if I would do him a favor. Anything, I responded. He asked if I would carry over a hundred thousand signatures, a petition he was spearheading, and deliver it to the Amazon headquarters in Seattle. The petition was to protect the sacred lands of a tribe in South Africa, a piece of land that Amazon was trying to develop. Without hesitation I agreed. I wore my cedar woven hat. I drove to downtown Seattle and met with the crew of activists Julian had put me in touch with. I was terrified and powerful at the same time when the doors to the Amazon building opened and a man in a suit, some slightly-higher-up, greeted me. I made him listen to the speech I prepared. I handed him the signatures. And I was proud in that moment that I could partake, at least in some small way, in the protection of sacred land, indigenous land.

As I sat writing poems about all of this, I let myself smile. I relaxed. I looked at the small blue church, angular and out of place, glaring at me through the afternoon sun. The church was a structure built by missionaries, by a group of people not of this land but who wished to gain control over it. When I let this imagery, the evidence of a colonized world, start to squeeze around my body like a rubber band, I try to remember my friend's face as we sat together in the canoe. I hear Julian's voice as he asked me to go boldly into the heart of the city and protest the development of sacred tribal lands across the world. I let these images take shape in me. I let them push me forward, through the weight of it, like a paddle slicing through water.

I watched as my partner began to paddle in from the lineup. The sun glittered along the surface and I looked down toward the hotels. I could see the crowded buildings that hugged the coastline, the resorts and shops in the distance. The second year my great-grandmother came to Hawai'i, she happened to be in one of those shops. By chance she ran into Pualani Kanaka'ole Kanahele there, the woman from the photos. She was delighted to see the woman who had inspired her on her previous trip, her first trip. Out of all the shops on the island, they both walked into this one. Grandma didn't believe this was a coincidence.

My partner was nearly to shore. I looked again toward Kona, the heart of downtown already buzzing with the hum of tourists anxious for white sand beaches and Blue Hawaiian cocktails. People who had traveled from the Midwest, from Sweden, and places even farther would soon pour out of the hotels and condos onto the small roads and beaches. I thought about how they will walk without thinking next to sacred places, ancient and powerful places. They will pass by sacred spaces on their way to spots called Snorkel Bob's and Magic Sands. I smiled when I remembered the white sand beach I stood on earlier that day, how my friend Kalei, a Native Hawaiian living here, back on their ancestral land, learning their traditional language and hula and chanting, was able to tell me when I asked, *But what is this beach really called?* The painted sign reads MAGIC SANDS. Kalei smiled and laughed a big laugh, because they understood my need to know. *It's not called Magic Sands!* And we both howled with laughter, because we were used to this kind of thing, the colonial tradition of giving names to places already named. But when Kalei told me the tourist-packed beach was once called La'aloa, I felt a heaviness in my heart, a desire to undo erasure, to erase every letter that was ever painted over a place that was already there. It means *very sacred*, Kalei added and hugged me immediately on the beach. Kalei's language teacher is the daughter of Pualani Kanaka'ole Kanahele, my great-grandmother's first friend in Hawai'i. I remembered the photo of the two women, taken over thirty years ago. I thought of my new friends. We have our own photos together. I thought of the kinships we were nurturing, the ways we will learn from each other in the future, the fact that I will always make this trip, as long as I am able to.

My partner climbed up the rocks where I sat. I watched as he wrung his hair out. He'd had a good surf session. He smiled when he saw that I hadn't even gotten into the water, despite the heat. I was busy writing, I told him. He nodded and sat next to me. He looked around, then back at me.

Did you know you're sitting on an ancient Hawaiian canoe launch? he said. I gasped. I looked ahead of me, at my bag, my notebook, the unused snorkel mask. I studied the black rock formations, the steps that led down into the water just beyond my bare feet. I nearly cried.

Of course I was. I closed my eyes and saw my great-grandmother's face. I let a few strands of hair coil around my fingers and gently pushed the offering into the cracked rock. *Tigʷičid*, I said, keeping my eyes on the water ahead and speaking the Lushootseed word for *thank you*.

Postscript

Louise's Spirit Song

I n February my partner drove us along a coastal road on the east side of the Big Island. When he made the turn onto the curved road that hugged the rocky shore, I gasped at the canopy of lush green above. The trees arched over us, draping vines and leaves across the narrow road. I asked Blaine to stop the car. This has always been one of my favorite intersections in nature: where forest meets the sea. It is written in my DNA to feel at home at this joining of nature. Water and tree line. Though I was an ocean away from my ancestral land in the Pacific Northwest, something about this road made me immediately less homesick.

Blaine pulled the car to the side of the road and I stepped out, grinning in the warm saltwater air. I had never seen anything so beautiful. Our trees are thick and sturdy, with wide trunks of old growth. I am used to the trails behind my home in Tacoma that blanket me in cedar boughs. Here the trees coiled and spindled in a lanky dance of wood and green.

As Blaine made his way to a trail through the forest, I stepped gently over the snaking roots along a path that led to the ocean ahead. I sat down on a large slab of rock, just through the trees and stared at the teal surface of water. When he found me, I wasn't sure if it had been five minutes or an hour. And when he asked me if I was okay, I smiled despite the warm flush of my face and the hot tears on my cheeks. He hugged me. Somehow, he knew in that moment that I missed her, my great-grandmother, more than I had this entire trip.

Two months after returning from the Big Island, I once again visited Grandma's language student. The dinner has become a tradition. I asked again if I could see the old photos of her in Hawaiʻi, that somehow it helped me feel closer to her, that she was still with us. My friend pulled out the usual stack of old photographs, and this time she had uncovered some that I hadn't seen before, discovered in some tucked-away box. As we shuffled the snapshots carefully in our hands, I stopped immediately when I recognized the same strange trees, the rocks ahead, and the ocean beyond. "I'm pretty sure I've been here, or close to here," I explained. At this my friend's face lit up and she told me a story she had never shared.

When my great-grandmother first landed on the Big Island, on that very first trip, her friend brought her here, to this stretch of forest and coastline. She wanted Grandma to see this place first. "She wanted to sit by the water," my friend went on, "so I left her to it and went on a walk as Vi sat on the rocks looking out at the ocean."

She returned to find my great-grandmother emotional; something had stirred her during her quiet meditation. When my friend asked Grandma what had happened, she responded, "I heard my mother's spirit song here."

I've been told the women in our family often hear our songs near water. My great-great-grandmother Louise Anderson had never been to Hawai'i. She had never been outside of the Pacific Northwest, her Coast Salish territory. But for some reason her spirit crossed an ocean, to find her daughter, my great-grandmother, on that beach, the first place she ever went when she arrived in Hawai'i. I looked down at the photograph. Grandma's back is toward the camera as she looks out into the waves. When my friend and I pulled up a map of the area and studied it, we used the landmarks, the things I could remember from my drive just two months earlier. According to the map and my memory, the mile markers and the beach parks, it was that exact same stretch of road where we pulled over. The photo could not have been taken more than a mile or two from where I'd sat.

I think of my great-great-grandmother's spirit song, how it traveled across an ocean to her daughter. And the songs on the cassette tape that Grandma Vi gave to the composer, instructing him to listen, to let the music guide him. She believed in sharing whatever strength can be found in these songs, that maybe it could heal something. I think of the song she must have heard every time she visited the island of Hawaiʻi, one that spoke of strength and revitalization, and the fight against erasure, against disappearing. All over the world, indigenous communities are fighting for their survival, the survival of their sacred lands, their languages, and stories. Communities are fighting for their land back, for the salmon to return, for a stop to the desecration of sacred sites. They are protecting tribal lands in South Africa. They are protecting Mauna Kea. They are water protectors and knowledge keepers, storytellers and healers.

They are the song the world needs right now.

Notes

*Orations – Excerpts in bold italics are taken from "Chief Seattle's 1854 Oration" – ver. 1 as it appears on the Suquamish Foundation website (suquamish.nsn.us)

"First Salmon Ceremony." In *Freeman's: Animals*, edited by John Freeman. New York: Grove, 2023.

"Thunder Song." In *There's a Revolution Outside, My Love: Letters from a Crisis*, edited by Tracy K. Smith and John Freeman. New York: Vintage, 2021.

"ʔuʔušəbicid čəd: An Indigenous Queer Love Story." *Yellow Medicine Review*, Spring 2022.

"The Jacket." *Hunger Mountain* 22: Everyday Chimeras, 2018.

"Cactus Flowers." *Orion*, Autumn 2022.

Acknowledgments

I'd like to acknowledge my use of the words of Chief SiʔaX̌' and honor the Duwamish and Suquamish people.

My hands go up in thanks to the wonderful cover artist, Maynard Johnny Jr. To have your work on this book is such a gift.

I want to thank my parents, Jill and John LaPointe, for their endless belief in me, and for reminding me of strength. My hands go up to the friends and family who made this book possible, including the Lushootseed Research Program and the incredible team at Counterpoint Press. I want to thank Nicole Caputo for your stunning design. To my editor, Harry, thank you for always being available for panicked phone calls, and for your time and guidance.

To Duvall, thank you for believing I had a book of essays in me, even when I doubted it.

To my kindred coven across the Pacific: Julian, Tayi, and Kalei, I cherish you all endlessly. Thank you for our connection, our stories, and all your love. To be in community with other radically proud indigenous authors and artists is what brings me back when things get hard.

I want to thank our dear family friend, Carolyn, for

the nights of beautiful conversations and food. Thank you for sharing the stories of your time with my great-grandma on the Big Island.

To my sister, Stacy, I will never forget that tree you snuck into my bedroom window at Christmas.Thank you for being the best sister.

To my brothers, Shain and Jermaine, thank you for being sweet and strong, and for constantly making me laugh when things felt too heavy, which in the writing of this book was often.

I want to thank Kari for the basement sessions and the late nights of practicing in my garage. Thank you for every song, for every performance and late-night recording session. You truly helped me learn to be loud.

Thank you, Anne and Ally, for road trips down the coast, for orca whales on ferries, and campfire poetry readings.

Thank you to my new poet family, for the Witch House where I was transformed by your love and strength.

And of course, to my beloved tropical sun worshiper, Blaine. Thank you for the support and nurturing, the care packages and the mountains of flowers that arrived whenever we were apart. When I was in the storm of this book you were my safe harbor. I love you to the moon and back.

Sasha taqʷšəblu LaPointe is a Coast Salish author from the Nooksack and Upper Skagit Indian tribes. She is the author of *Red Paint: The Ancestral Autobiography of a Coast Salish Punk*, winner of a Pacific Northwest Book Award and an NPR Best Book of the year. She received a double MFA in creative nonfiction and poetry from the Institute of American Indian Arts. She lives in Tacoma, Washington. Find out more at sasha-lapointe.com.